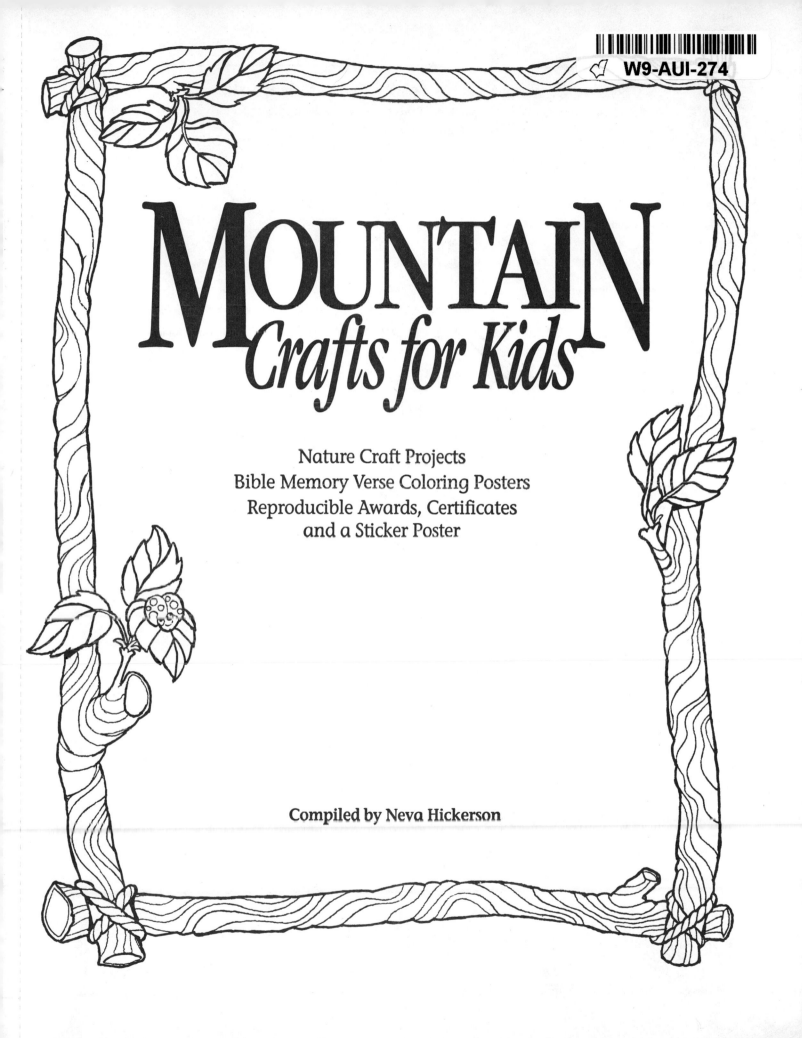

MOUNTAIN
Crafts for Kids

Nature Craft Projects
Bible Memory Verse Coloring Posters
Reproducible Awards, Certificates
and a Sticker Poster

Compiled by Neva Hickerson

How to make clean copies from this book.

You may make copies of portions of this book with a clean conscience if:

➤ you (or someone in your organization) are the original purchaser.

➤ you are using the copies you make for a noncommercial purpose
(such as teaching or promoting a ministry) within your church or organization.

➤ You follow the instructions provided in this book.

However, it is *illegal* for you to make copies if:

➤ you are using the material to promote, advertise or sell a product or service other than for ministry fund-raising.

➤ you are using the material in or on a product for sale.

➤ you or your organization are **not** the original purchaser of this book.

By following these guidelines you help us keep our products affordable. Thank you.

Gospel Light

Neva Hickerson, Editor • **Christy Weir**, Consulting Editor • **Phyllis Atchison**, Assistant Editor • **Marla Burke, Patty Hambrick, Brenda Kilgore, Lynnette Pennings, Dianne Rowell, Susan Stegenga, Kim Sullivan**, Contributing Writers • **Gwen Decker, Eddi Fredrick, Sheryl Haystead,** Contributing Editors • **Carolyn Gillmon**, Designer • **Chizuko Yasuda**, Illustrator

Library of Congress Cataloging-in-Publication Data
Hickerson, Neva.
    Mountain crafts for kids: nature craft projects, Bible memory
verse coloring posters, reproducible awards, certificates, and a
sticker poster / compiled by Neva Hickerson; [Marla Burke...et al.,
contributing writers; Chizuko Yasuda, illustrator].
        p.   cm.
    Includes index.
ISBN 0-8307-1476-6 :
    1. Creative activities and seat work—Handbooks, manuals, etc.
2. Teaching—Aids and devices—Handbooks, manuals, etc. I. Title.
LB1027.25.H53   1992
372.13—dc20   91-30885
                                                            CIP

Contents

Introduction to *Mountain Crafts for Kids* 4
Crafts with a Message 5
Bible Verse Messages for Crafts 6
Backpack Projects 7
Drying and Pressing Leaves and Flowers 8
Preparing to Do Crafts 9
Helpful Hints 10

Section One
Crafts for Young Children 11

Sponge-Painted Backpack 12
Twig Trees 12
Backwoods Bug Jar 13
Rock Owl 14
Forest Animal Hats 14
Raccoon Blinker 16
Leaf Place Mat 18
Colored-Pebble Picture 19
Nature Wall Hanging 19
Plant a Tree! 20

Section Two
Crafts for Younger Elementary 21

Stenciled Backpack 22
Ladybug Tic-Tac-Toe 24
Nature Collage Picture Frame 25
Spatter-Painted Bandana 26
Finger Puppets 26
Bear Paw Stilts 28
Owl with Revolving Eyes 30
Pressed Flower Sun Catcher 32
Rock Campfire Scene 32
Pinecone Rabbit 34

Section Three
Crafts for Older Elementary 35

Tic-Tac-Toe Backpack 36
Rickrack Backpack 36

Flowering Tiles 37
Nature Image Plaque 37
Pop-Up Frog 38
Helpless Hiker Paperweight 40
Forest Animal Mobile 40
Mountain View Diorama 42
  Background Scene 42
  Trees and Shrubs 43
  Tent and Campfire 43
  Beaver and Beaver Dam 44
  Fisherman and Canoe 44
Tree Branch Frame 45
Secret Stone 46
Leaf-Covered Box 47
Really Neat Recycling Bins 48
Embossed Metal Magnets 48
Pop-Up Bear Card 50
Somethin' Fishy Wrist Game 53
Nature Checkers Game 54

Section Four
Crafts for Junior High 55

Appliquéd Backpack 56
Wax Leaf Wreath 56
Granite Bookends 57
Dried Flower Swag 58
Molded Sawdust Animal 59
Pinecone Basket 59
Weather Stone 60
Forest Frame 61
Pop-Up Butterfly 62
Lashed Trivet 66

Section Five
Reproducible Pages 67

Bible Memory Verse Coloring Pages 69-107
  For Younger Elementary 69-87
  For Older Elementary 89-107
Certificates, Awards, Sticker Posters 109-117
Index 119

Introduction to *Mountain Crafts for Kids*

God's Wonderful Creation

Children are naturally curious about the world of nature. They're fascinated by a giant Sequoia towering above, and delight in watching a hairy spider creeping across the path below. The infinite variety found in God's creation was the inspiration for this resource book of nature crafts, *Mountain Crafts for Kids*. Many crafts call for materials found in the mountains (or in your own backyard) such as pinecones, leaves, stones, and twigs. Other projects center around animals, insects and plants found in the mountains. Still others encourage recycling and being good stewards of God's creation.

We hope that you and your students enjoy learning about the great outdoors as you complete projects from *Mountain Crafts for Kids*. These crafts can help children experience a sense of wonder at God's creation and be inspired to help protect wild places so they can be enjoyed for generations to come.

Don't Feel Confined!

We encourage you to see *Mountain Crafts for Kids* as a foundation for your craft program. Then, see yourself, the parent, teacher or craft director, as an essential element in planning enjoyable and successful craft projects for children and youth.

Don't feel confined to the crafts in a particular age-level section. You may want to adapt a craft from a younger or older age level.

In addition, don't feel confined by the materials listed for crafts. Consider what materials you have on hand, what materials are available in your area and what materials you can afford to purchase. In some cases you will be able to substitute materials in order to use something you already have.

Have Fun!

What can you do to make sure craft time is successful and fun for your students? First, remember the process is as important as the final product. Provide a variety of materials with which children may work. Allow children to make choices and be creative. Don't expect every child's project to turn out the same. Don't insist that children "stay in the lines."

Second, choose projects that are appropriate for the skill level of your students. This will increase the likelihood that students will be successful and satisfied with their finished products.

Finally, show an interest in the unique way each child approaches a project and affirm the choices he or she has made. The ability to create is part of being made in the image of God, the Creator!

"Outdoor Life" Sections

Each craft in this book includes a section entitled "Outdoor Life." These sections are designed to help you enhance craft times with interesting facts and discussions. They include information and questions about mountain plant and animal life, recycling and protection of wilderness areas. If your crafts program includes large groups of children, you may want to share these conversation suggestions with each helper who can in turn use them with individuals or small groups.

Crafts with a Message

Many of the projects in *Mountain Crafts for Kids* can easily become crafts with a message. Children can create slogans or poetry as part of their projects. Or, you can provide an appropriate poem, thought or Bible verse for children to attach to their crafts.

On the following page you will find Bible verses relating to the mountains and God's creation. You may want to photocopy one or more of these verses and incorporate them into your craft projects. Additional verses may be taken from the coloring posters on pages 69-107.

Tree Branch Frame

"Let the rivers clap their hands, let the mountains sing together for joy." Psalm 98:8

Leaf Place Mat

A Poem About Leaves

Nature Collage Picture Frame

"I praise you because I am fearfully and wonderfully made." Psalm 139:14

Appliquéd Backpack

Save the Brown Bear

Bible Verse Messages for Crafts

"Let the rivers clap their hands, let the mountains sing together for joy." Psalm 98:8

"How beautiful on the mountains are the feet of those who bring good news." Isaiah 52:7

"He who forms the mountains, creates the wind, and reveals his thoughts to man, he who turns dawn to darkness, and treads the high places of the earth— the Lord God Almighty is his name." Amos 4:13

"The righteous will thrive like a green leaf." Proverbs 11:28

"As the deer pants for streams of water, so my soul pants for you, O God." Psalm 42:1

"I praise you because I am fearfully and wonderfully made; your works are wonderful, I know that full well." Psalm 139:14

"Blessed is the man...[whose] delight is in the law of the Lord.... He is like a tree planted by streams of water, which yields its fruit in season and whose leaf does not wither." Psalms 1:1-3

"God saw all that he had made, and it was very good." Genesis 1:31

Backpack Projects

Mountain Crafts for Kids includes five different backpack projects (see Contents). These simple backpacks are constructed ahead of time by adults and then decorated by students. The students may keep the backpacks for their own use or they may choose to fill the decorated backpacks with school supplies or toiletries and arrange to give them to needy children.

Below are instructions for making a simple backpack to be used with any of the backpack projects described in *Mountain Crafts for Kids.*

Materials: Scissors, thread, pins, measuring tape, sewing machine. For each backpack—1/3 yard (30 cm) solid color, heavy cotton fabric; 2 inches (5 cm) of Velcro; approximately 1⅓ yards (50 cm) of 1-inch (2.5cm) nylon webbing.

Instructions:
• Preshrink fabric.

• Cut a 12x30-inch (30x75-cm) rectangle from fabric (sketch a).

• Cut webbing into two 20-inch (50-cm) lengths.

• Fold fabric rectangle in half. Place the lengths of nylon webbing inside folded fabric as shown (sketch b). Pin nylon webbing in place as you pin sides of backpack together.

• Stitch sides of backpack. Trim seams and clip corners (sketch c). Turn backpack right side out.

• Turn top edge of backpack under twice and stitch.

• Separate Velcro pieces. Stitch pieces inside the top edge of backpack, centered and facing each other (sketch d).

• Pin free ends of nylon webbing to back inner edge on either side of Velcro (sketch d). Adjust webbing straps according to size of child who will be using backpack. Stitch webbing in place.

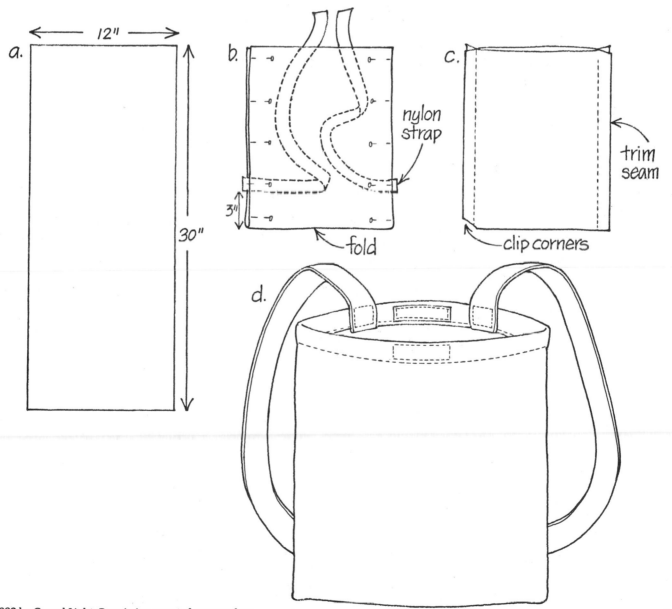

Drying and Pressing Leaves and Flowers

Mountain Crafts for Kids includes various projects requiring pressed or dried nature items (see Contents). Below are instructions for drying and pressing your own leaves, grasses, ferns, herbs and flowers.

Pressing Leaves, Grasses, Ferns and Flowers:

• Pick fresh leaves, ferns, grasses and flowers. (Please be sensitive to the fact that it is illegal to pick wildflowers in some places.)

• Lay each item separately (not touching or overlapping) on several sheets of newspaper.

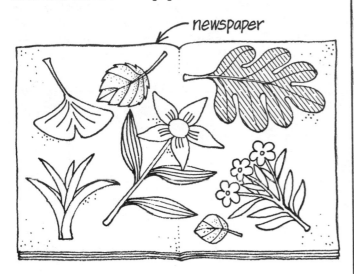

newspaper

• Cover the nature items with more newspapers and weight down with heavy objects such as books. The newspaper will absorb moisture from the items being pressed. (For especially "juicy" flowers, place a layer of paper towels between flowers and newspapers.)

• Set in a cool, dry area such as a garage or basement.

• Green leaves and fresh flowers should be pressed for about a month. Leaves that have already turned color need to be pressed for about two weeks. If materials are removed before they are completely dried, the edges will curl.

Alternate Drying Method for Leaves, Ferns and Grasses:

• Place leaves between two sheets of wax paper. Place a layer of newspaper under and over wax paper.

• Press with a warm iron. The wax from the paper will melt and coat both sides of the leaf.

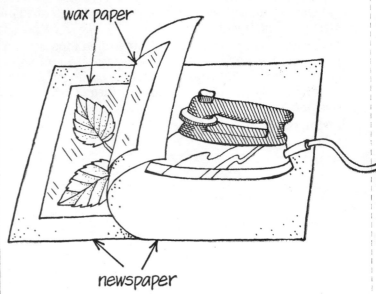

wax paper

newspaper

• Remove the leaves, let cool, then press overnight between the pages of a heavy book.

Air-Drying Flowers and Herbs:

• Hang flowers upside-down in small bunches, with stems tied together. (Large, pulpy plants should be hung separately.)

• Hang in warm, dark, dry place.

• Dry for two or three weeks.

• When dry, spray flowers and herbs with a clear acrylic spray as a preservative to prevent moisture in the air from making them limp again.

Preparing to Do Crafts

• If you are planning to use crafts with a child at home, here are three helpful tips:

1. Focus on the projects in the section for your child's age, but don't ignore projects that are listed for older or younger ages. Elementary age children enjoy many of the projects grouped under "Crafts for Young Children" and they can do them with little or no adult assistance. And younger children are always interested in doing "big kid" things. Just plan on working along with the child, helping with tasks the child cannot handle alone.

2. Start with projects which call for materials you have around the house. Make a list of items you do not have which are needed for projects you think your child will enjoy. Plan to gather those supplies in one expedition.

3. If certain materials seem too difficult to obtain, a little thought can usually lead to appropriate substitutions. And often the homemade version ends up being a real improvement over the original plan.

• If you are planning to lead a group of children in doing craft projects, keep these hints in mind:

1. Choose projects which will allow children to work with a variety of materials.

2. Make your selection of all projects far enough in advance to allow time to gather all needed supplies in one coordinated effort. Many projects use some of the same items.

3. Make up a sample of each project to be sure the directions are fully understood and potential problems can be avoided. You may find you will want to adapt some projects to simplify procedures or vary the materials required.

4. Many items can be acquired as donations from people or businesses if you plan ahead and make your needs known. Many churches distribute lists of materials needed to their congregation and community and are able to provide crafts at little or no cost. Some items can be brought by the children themselves.

5. In making your supplies list, distinguish between items which every individual child will need and those which will be shared among a group.

6. Keep in mind that some materials may be shared among more than one age level, but only if there is good coordination among the groups. It is extremely frustrating to a teacher to expect to have scissors, only to discover another group is using them. Basic supplies which are used repeatedly in craft projects should usually be provided to every group.

Helpful Hints

Using Glue with Young Children

Since preschoolers have difficulty using glue bottles effectively, you may want to try one of the following procedures. Purchase glue in large containers (up to one gallon size).

a. Pour small amount of glue into several shallow containers.

b. Dilute glue by mixing a little water into each container.

c. Children use paste brushes to spread glue on project.

OR

a. Pour a small amount of glue into a plastic margarine tub.

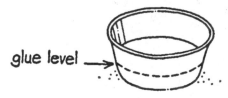

b. Give each child a cotton swab. The child dips the cotton swab into the glue and rubs glue on project.

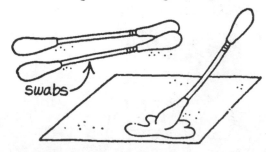

c. Excess glue can be poured back into the large container at the end of each session.

How to Make Patterns

You will need: Tissue paper, lightweight cardboard, pencil, scissors.

a. Trace pattern from book onto tissue paper.

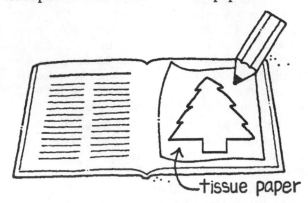

b. Cut out tissue paper pattern and trace onto cardboard.

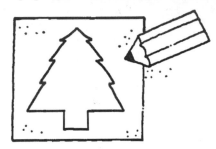

c. Cut out cardboard pattern.

Cutting with Scissors

When cutting with scissors is required for these crafts, take note of the fact that some of the children in your class may be left-handed. It is very difficult for a left-handed person to cut with scissors that were designed to be used with the right hand. Have available in your classroom two or three pairs of left-handed scissors. These can be obtained from a school supply center.

Section One/Ages 3-5

Crafts for Young Children

Craft projects for young children are a blend of, "I wanna do it myself!" and "I need help!" Each project, because it is intended to come out looking like a recognizable something, usually requires a certain amount of adult assistance—in preparing a pattern, in doing some cutting, in preselecting magazine pictures, in using the iron, etc. The younger the child, the more the adult will need to do, but care must always be taken not to rob the child of the satisfaction of his or her own unique efforts. Neither must the adult's desire to have a nice finished project override the child's pleasure at experimenting with color and texture. Avoid the temptation to do the project for the child or to improve on the child's efforts.

Some of the crafts have enrichment and simplification ideas included with them. An enrichment idea provides a way to make the craft more challenging for the older child. A simplification idea helps the younger child complete the craft more successfully. If you find a child frustrated with some of the limitations of working on a structured craft—although most of the projects in this book allow plenty of leeway for children to be themselves—it may be a signal the child needs an opportunity to work with more creative, less structured materials: blank paper and paints, play dough, or abstract collages (gluing miscellaneous shapes or objects onto surfaces such as paper, cardboard or anything else to which glue will adhere). Remember the cardinal rule of thumb in any task a young child undertakes: the process the child goes through is more important than the finished product.

Sponge-Painted Backpack

(ONE-DAY PROJECT/30 MINUTES)

Note: This craft requires a simple fabric backpack for each child. For backpack materials and sewing instructions see page 7.

Materials: Various colors of fabric paint, shallow pans for paint, sponges, clothespins, scissors, newspapers, iron, ironing board, water. For each child—one backpack.

Preparation: Cut damp sponges into simple shapes such as circles, triangles, rectangles and squares. Attach a clothespin to each sponge shape. Cover work surface with newspapers. Pour or squeeze paint into shallow pans.

Instruct each child in the following procedures:

• Dip sponge shape into paint (sketch a) and then press onto front of backpack. Repeat, using different shapes and colors, to create design (sketch b).

• Allow to dry for at least four hours. Then adult should iron back of painted fabric to set paint.

Enrichment Idea: Show children how they can use shapes to create trees, a mountain and a sun (see sketch).

Outdoor Life: Hold up triangle-shaped sponge and ask, **What shape is this? What are some things we might see in the mountains that are shaped like a triangle?** (Trees, mountains, tents.) Hold up circle-shaped sponge and ask, **What shape is this? What are some things we might see in the mountains that are shaped like a circle?** (Sun, pond, stone, animal's eyes.)

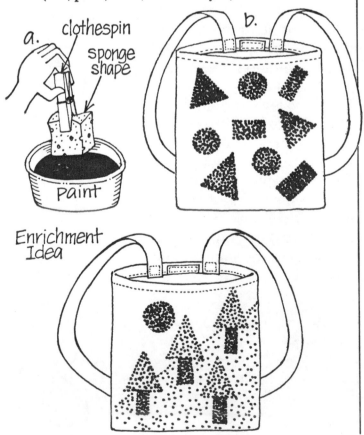

Twig Trees

(ONE-DAY PROJECT/30 MINUTES)

Materials: Twigs, glue, brightly-colored construction paper, felt pens.

Preparation: For younger children, use felt pens to outline simple tree shapes on construction paper—one for each child (sketch a). Leave room on page for children to create their own designs with twigs.

Instruct each child in the following procedures:

• Older children use felt pen to draw a few triangular tree shapes on paper (sketch a).

• Select twigs and break to appropriate length, if necessary.

• Glue twigs onto tree outline.

• Glue additional twigs on paper to create a mountain scene as in sketch b. (Ideas: mountains, hikers, sun, stream.)

Enrichment Ideas: Cut triangle shapes from green (solid or print) fabric which children may glue onto tree shapes before outlining with twigs (see sketch).

Outdoor Life: Take children on a walk outside to look at the trees. **Which is the tallest tree? The shortest? Which tree has the biggest leaves? The smallest? Trees are the biggest and strongest of all plants!**

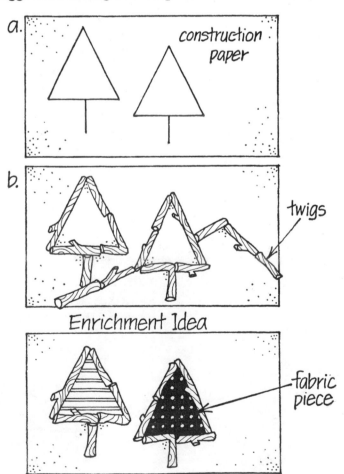

Backwoods Bug Jar

(ONE-DAY PROJECT/30 MINUTES)

Materials: Circle Pattern, window screen, colored tissue paper, green construction paper, cardboard, scissors, ruler, pencil, glue, black permanent marker, hammer and nail or drill, damp paper towels. For each child—one plastic peanut butter or instant coffee jar with a 2¾-inch (6.9-cm) neck, standard size mason jar band, one chenille wire.

Preparation: Trace Circle Pattern onto cardboard and cut out. Trace cardboard circle onto screen and cut out—one for each child. Use nail or drill to make two small holes opposite each other near the top of each jar (sketch a). Cut colored tissue paper into 2x4-inch (5x10-cm) rectangles—approximately eight for each child. Cut green construction paper into 1x4-inch (2.5x10-cm) strips—three for each child.

Instruct each child in the following procedures:
- Glue screen to the inside of the mason jar band. Let dry.
- Use scissors to cut blades of grass in green construction paper strips (sketch b).
- Glue grass around the bottom of the jar. (Strips will overlap.)
- Crumple tissue pieces to form flowers.
- Glue flowers to the grass on jar (sketch c).
- With teacher's help, poke ends of chenille wire through the holes in the jar. Bend the ends of the chenille wire inside of jar to keep it from slipping out.
- Use a damp towel to clean excess glue off jar.
- Using permanent marker, teacher letters "Bugs" on the side of the jar (sketch c).
- Collect bugs to keep in jar. Be sure to provide your bugs with leaves and water.
- Screw on the bug jar lid.

Enrichment Ideas: Older children may enjoy using tissue paper and twist ties to make butterflies, snails and spiders (see sketches). **To make butterfly:** Place a twist tie around the middle of a piece of tissue paper. Twist the tie together several times. Curl the tips of the tie to make antennas. **To make snail:** Twist piece of tissue paper into a rope. Coil the rope to make a snail shell. Fold twist tie in half and place around bottom of coiled tissue. Twist ends of twist tie to make antennas. **To make spider:** Cut two twist ties in half. Twist the four pieces together in the middle and bend to make legs. Crumple a piece of tissue for body. Glue body to legs. Glue butterflies, snails and spiders to jar or place inside jar.

Outdoor Life: When it's cold outside, what do you do to keep warm? It can become very cold in the mountains, but the insects who live there don't put on coats or turn on the heat. The grasshoppers, beetles and butterflies that live in the mountains have a special chemical in their blood to help them stay warm in the cold mountain air.

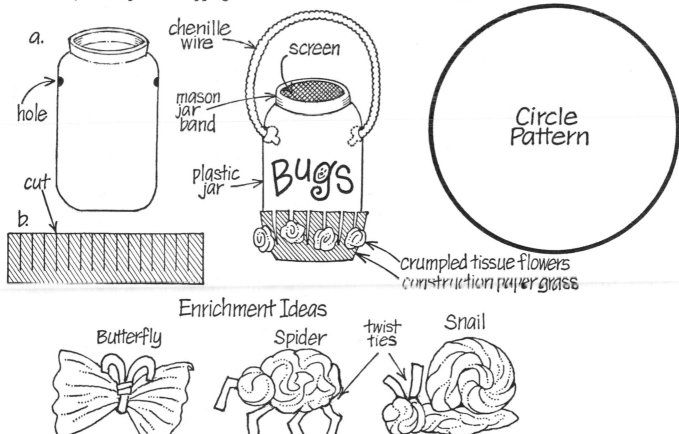

a. hole / cut

b.

chenille wire / screen / mason jar band / plastic jar / Bugs

Circle Pattern

crumpled tissue flowers
construction paper grass

Enrichment Ideas

Butterfly / Spider / twist ties / Snail

Rock Owl
(ONE-DAY PROJECT/30 MINUTES)

Materials: Tacky glue, heavy-duty scissors or wire cutters. For each child—one flat, oblong rock approximately 3 inches (7.5 cm) long, two three-pronged twigs for owl's feet, two acorn tops, three pinecone petals, six to eight soft feathers approximately 2 inches (5 cm) in length.

Preparation: Wash rocks and allow to dry. Cut petals from pinecones. Stems may need to be cut from acorn tops to create flat surfaces for gluing.

Instruct each child in the following procedures:
- Glue feathers to rock to cover front side.
- Glue acorn tops (stem side down) near top of rock for eyes.
- Glue pinecone petals above eyes for ears.
- Glue small pinecone petal beneath eyes for beak.
- Glue twigs to bottom of rock for feet. Let dry.

Outdoor Life: **What sound does an owl make? Most owls live in homes made inside tree trunks. They sleep during the day and stay awake at night. When owls fly, they are very quiet, making almost no sound.**

pinecone petals

acorn top

feather

twig

Forest Animal Hats
(ONE-DAY PROJECT/30 MINUTES)

Materials: Fox, Raccoon, Beaver Hat Patterns, measuring stick, lightweight cardboard, butcher paper, black felt pen, scissors, crayons, stapler and staples.

Preparation: Using Forest Animal Hat Patterns as guides, draw each hat onto cardboard and cut out. Trace Patterns onto butcher paper and cut out—one for each child. (Children will select one animal from the three choices provided.) Use black felt pen to draw features on each animal (sketch a). Eye and ear features should be drawn on front side of hat. Mouth and nose features should be drawn on backside of hat. Tail features should be drawn on front and back sides of hat.

Instruct each child in the following procedures:
- Select a hat and color it.
- Fold down nose.
- With teacher's help, staple hat to fit your head (sketch b).

Enrichment Idea: Use heavy art paper for hats. Children use water colors or tempera paints to decorate.

Outdoor Life: Check out library books containing pictures of a fox, a beaver and a raccoon. Show pictures and invite children to identify the animals. **Beavers have strong, sharp teeth which they use to cut bark off trees. Bark is their favorite food! Beavers also use their sharp teeth to cut down trees. They use the trees for building dams across streams.**

a.

b.

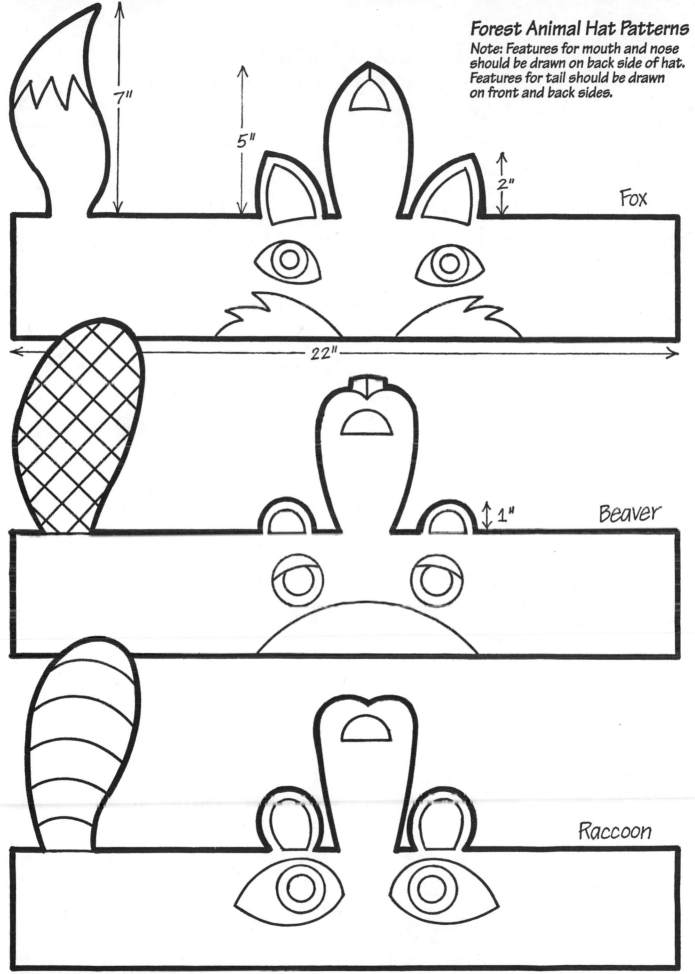

Forest Animal Hat Patterns
Note: Features for mouth and nose should be drawn on back side of hat. Features for tail should be drawn on front and back sides.

7"

5"

2"

Fox

22"

1"

Beaver

Raccoon

Raccoon Blinker

(ONE-DAY PROJECT/30 MINUTES)

Materials: Raccoon Head and Eye/Tongue Patterns, white card-stock paper, scissors, felt pens or crayons, photocopier. For each child—one ¾-inch (1.9-cm) paper fastener (brad).

Preparation: Photocopy Raccoon Head and Eye/Tongue Patterns onto white card stock—one for each child. For younger children, cut out patterns ahead of time. Make a sample Raccoon.

Instruct each child in the following procedures:
• Cut out Raccoon Head and Eye/Tongue pieces.
• Color Raccoon head and tongue.

• With teacher's help, poke paper fastener through "x" on Raccoon head and eyes. Open paper fastener to secure (sketch a).
• Move tongue to make Raccoon's eyes look in different directions (sketch b).

Outdoor Life: Have you ever seen a raccoon? Raccoons live in the woods. If you live near the woods, a raccoon may come into your yard at night. Native Americans told stories about raccoons, calling them "the black-masked little bear." Raccoons are known for being curious, smart and playful.

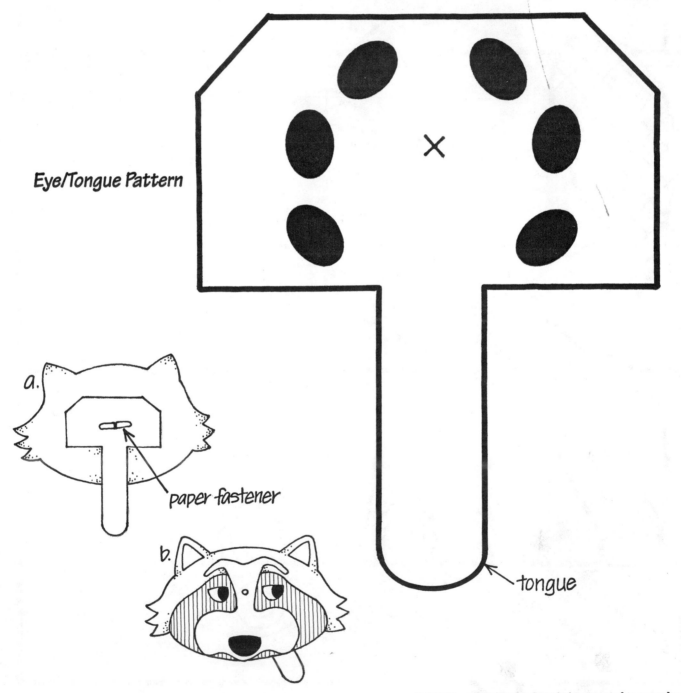

Eye/Tongue Pattern

a.

paper fastener

b.

tongue

Colored-Pebble Picture

(ONE-DAY PROJECT/30 MINUTES)

Materials: Pebbles, four or more colors of acrylic paint or spray paint, plastic or Styrofoam cups, twigs, glue in squeeze bottles, felt pens, newspapers, hole punch, yarn, scissors, ruler. For each child—one sturdy paper plate.

Preparation: Cut yarn into 10-inch (25-cm) lengths—one for each child. Wash pebbles, if necessary, and allow to dry. Paint pebbles in either of these ways:

- Spray paint: Spread a number of pebbles out on a newspaper and use spray paint. Make at least four different colors. Turn pebbles once or twice while drying to avoid sticking. Some colors may need two coats. Allow to dry overnight.

- Acrylic paint: Put a number of pebbles in the bottom of a cup, pour a small amount of paint over them, stir with a twig to coat all sides. Pour pebbles out onto newspaper to dry. Make at least four different colors. Turn or flip pebbles during drying to avoid sticking. Allow to dry overnight.

Instruct each child in the following procedures:
- Squeeze glue onto plate to draw a design.
- Place pebbles on top of glued design. Let dry.
- Use felt pens to add details to picture, if desired.
- With teacher's help, punch two holes in the top of plate. Thread yarn through holes and tie for hanger.

Enrichment Ideas: In addition to pebbles, children use a variety of nature items, such as pinecone petals, twigs and dried flowers to create a collage.

Outdoor Life: Play a guessing game with the children saying, **I'm thinking of something that is gray and can fit in my hand. It is very hard. Do you know what it is?** (A rock.) **Did you know that most of the earth is made of rock? If we could dig a hole, very deep into the ground, eventually we would find rock. The pebbles we used in our pictures are tiny rocks.**

Nature Wall Hanging

(ONE-DAY PROJECT/30 MINUTES)

Materials: Pressed or dried flowers (see "Drying and Pressing Leaves and Flowers," p. 8), earth-tone air-drying clay, ⅛-inch (.3-cm) suede strips, scissors, glue, glue gun and glue sticks. For each child—several pieces of dried bark.

Preparation: Use scissors to cut suede strips into 4-inch (10-cm) lengths—one for each child.

Instruct each child in the following procedures:
- Select several pieces of dried bark. With teacher's help, glue pieces together to form base for wall hanging (sketch a). Glue suede strip to back of bark for hanger.
- Choose an assortment of flowers and arrange them on bark base. Glue in place.
- Press a small ball of clay over the flower stems (sketch b).
- Allow clay to dry overnight. (As clay dries, it may pull away from wood. Teacher should use glue gun to reattach dried clay to bark, if necessary.)

Simplification Idea: Use a wooden shingle instead of bark pieces.

Outdoor Life: If possible, take children outside where they can see and touch the bark of a tree. **Tree trunks are covered with a layer of wood called bark. Why do you think a tree has bark? The bark stops the tree from losing water and protects the tree from getting hurt. Bark is a dead layer of the tree. When the tree grows bigger the bark doesn't grow. Instead, it splits and cracks and sometimes falls on the ground. Never strip bark off a tree. If the bark is damaged, the tree might die.**

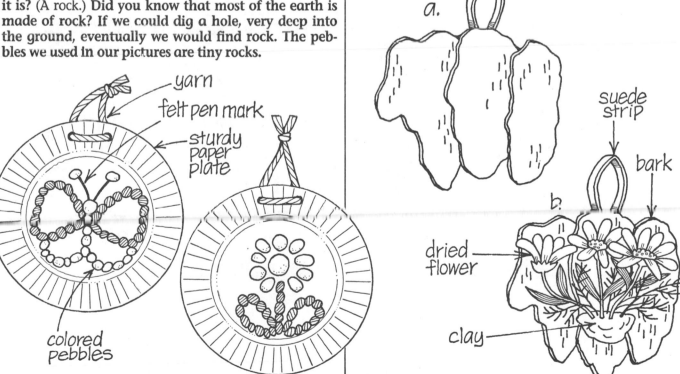

Plant a Tree!

(ONE-DAY PROJECT/30 MINUTES)

Materials: "How to Grow a Tree" instructions, potting soil, gravel, trowels, large spoons, water, newspaper, brown paper bags, brightly-colored construction paper, glue, pencil, scissors, craft knife, transparent tape, measuring stick, paper, photocopier. For each child—a half-gallon milk carton, one pine or spruce seedling.

Preparation: Use craft knife to cut milk cartons to 4-inch (10-cm) height. Cut paper bags into 5x16-inch (12.5x40-cm) strips—one for each child. Cover work area with newspapers. Photocopy "How to Grow a Tree" instructions and cut out—one for each child.

Instruct each child in the following procedures:
- With teacher's help, wrap paper bag strip around milk carton. Secure with tape. Fold edges to inside of carton.
- Glue "How to Grow a Tree" instructions to one side of planter for parents' information.
- Cut shapes from construction paper and glue to bag to decorate planter.
- Use spoon to place a layer of gravel in bottom of milk carton.
- Use trowel to fill milk carton with soil.
- Dig a hole in the center of soil and place seedling in it.
- Sprinkle a spoonful of soil over roots and pat down.
- Water seedling.

Outdoor Life: Why do you think God made trees? (They give fruit, shade, wood, beauty, etc.) **Trees also help to make cool, clean air for everyone to breathe. Ask your parents to help you take care of this tree and when it is ready, to plant it outside. By planting a tree, you are helping to make the world a better place to live!**

How to Grow a Tree
- Keep seedling in a sunny spot.
- Lightly water daily.
- When seedling is 5-6 inches (7.5-10 cm) tall, transplant it outside where tree will have room to grow.
- Water young tree during dry spells and make sure other plants do not cover it.

Section Two/Grades 1-2
Crafts for Younger Elementary

Children in the first few years of school are delights to work with in completing craft projects. They have a handle on most of the basic skills needed, they are eager to do things and their taste in art has usually not yet surpassed their ability to produce. In other words, they generally like the things they make.

Since reading ability is not a factor in most craft projects, crafts can be a great leveler among a group. Some children excel here who may or may not be top achievers in other areas.

Many of the projects in the section for young children also will appeal to younger elementary children.

Stenciled Backpack
(ONE-DAY PROJECT/30 MINUTES)

Note: This craft requires a simple fabric backpack for each child. For Backpack materials and sewing instructions see page 7.

Materials: Leaf Stencil Patterns, craft knife, tagboard, scissors, pencil, tissue paper, various colors of fabric paint, paintbrushes, shallow pans for paint, newspapers, iron, ironing board. For each child—one backpack.

Preparation: Make Leaf Stencils following instructions on page 23—one set for every three or four children. Cover work surface with newspapers. Pour or squeeze paint into shallow pans.

Instruct each child in the following procedures:
• Lay stencil on front side of backpack and carefully paint within cutout area. Repeat using other stencils and colors to create design.

• Allow to dry for at least four hours. Then adult should iron back of painted fabric to set paint.

Enrichment Idea: Allow children to use purchased alphabet stencils to paint names or messages on backpacks.

Outdoor Life: Show a magazine picture or photograph of a beautiful mountain scene. **How many of you would like to visit a place like this? Imagine that there are cola cans floating down the stream and trash laying on the ground. Do you think it would still be a nice place to visit? You can help keep wild places clean. When you visit the mountains, carry your trash home in a backpack and put it in a trash can or recycling bin, where it belongs!**

Enrichment
Idea

Rebecca

Leaf Stencil Patterns

To make a stencil: Trace stencil pattern onto tissue paper and cut out. Lay tissue paper pattern on tagboard, cardboard or bristol board (available at graphic art supply stores) and trace. Use craft knife to cut out shapes, leaving outer area intact. Students lay stencil on craft project and carefully paint within the cutout area. You may want to trace actual leaves to create additional stencil patterns of your own.

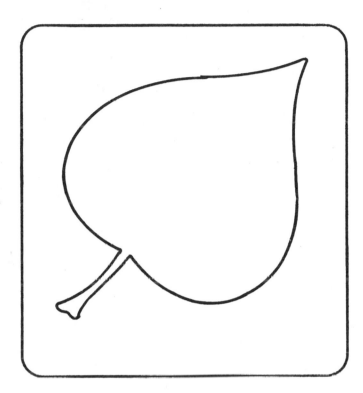

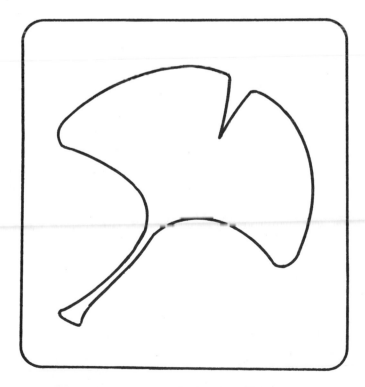

Ladybug Tic-Tac-Toe

(TWO-DAY PROJECT/30 MINUTES EACH DAY)

Materials: White foam core (available at graphic art supply stores) or poster board, green and red acrylic paint, paintbrushes, tacky glue, fresh picked leaves, permanent black felt pens, ruler, sheets of scratch paper, newspapers, shallow containers for paint, craft knife. For each child—10 smooth-surfaced stones approximately 1 inch (2.5 cm) in diameter, four straight twigs approximately 8 inches (20 cm) long.

Preparation: Wash stones and leaves, if necessary, and allow to dry. Use craft knife to cut foam core or poster board into 10-inch (25-cm) squares for game board—one for each child. Pour paint into shallow containers. Cover work surface with newspapers.

Instruct each child in the following procedures:

DAY ONE:
- Paint stones red. Let dry. (They may need two coats.)
- Choose a leaf and paint it green on one side. Pick up leaf by stem and lay painted side down on a sheet of scratch paper. Lay another sheet of paper on top of leaf and gently press down with hand to get rid of excess paint (do not rub back and forth).
- Pick up leaf again and lay painted side down on foam core game board, cover with a clean sheet of paper and gently press down (sketch a). Repeat process of printing leaf shapes on game board until desired look is achieved. Allow to dry overnight.

DAY TWO:
- Use felt pen to draw spots and lines on rocks to make five male and five female ladybugs (sketch b).
- Glue twigs to game board to make Tic-Tac-Toe grid (sketch c). Allow to dry.
- Game is ready to play.

Outdoor Life: Did you know that ladybugs are helpful insects? Ladybugs have very big appetites. They eat insects that are harmful to plants and trees. In fact, just twelve ladybugs can save a fruit tree from being ruined by insect pests. Ladybugs are nice to have around!

a. foam core game board

b. painted stones

c. twigs / painted game board

Three ladybugs in a row!

Nature Collage Picture Frame

(ONE- OR TWO-DAY PROJECT/60 MINUTES)

Materials: Frame Pattern, instant camera and film, burlap, yarn or ¼-inch (.6-cm) ribbon, ruler, scissors, cardboard, tacky glue, small nature items (tiny pinecones, petals from larger pinecones, dried pine needles, dried weeds, dried flowers, seed pods, pebbles, etc.).

See "Drying and Pressing Leaves and Flowers," page 8. For each child—one basket-type paper plate holder.

Optional: Standard camera and film.

Preparation: Trace Frame Pattern onto cardboard and cut out—one for each child.

Trace Frame Pattern onto burlap and cut out—one for each child.

Cut ribbon or yarn into 10-inch (25-cm) lengths—one for each child.

Use an instant camera to take a close-up photograph of each child.

Optional: Use standard camera to take photos in advance and have pictures developed in time to complete craft.

Instruct each child in the following procedures:

• Glue burlap circle to cardboard circle.

• Glue photo to the center of the paper plate holder.

• Glue burlap-covered cardboard circle over picture to frame it.

• Decorate frame by gluing nature items to paper plate holder. With teacher's help, tie pieces of ribbon or yarn around bunches of dried weeds and straw flowers to make miniature bouquets. Glue onto paper plate holder. Let dry.

• Weave a 10-inch (25-cm) length of yarn or ribbon through top of paper plate holder and tie ends securely to make a hanger for the frame.

Enrichment Idea: Children go on a nature hike to collect items for their collages.

Outdoor Life: Let's pretend we're taking a hike in the mountains. What very big things do you think we'd see? Very small things? Moving things?

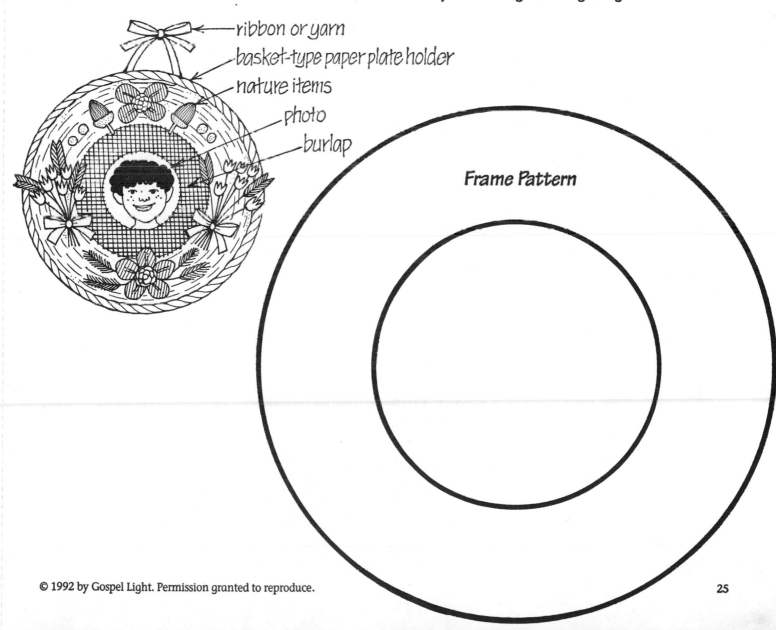

ribbon or yarn
basket-type paper plate holder
nature items
photo
burlap

Frame Pattern

Spatter-Painted Bandana

(ONE-DAY PROJECT/30 MINUTES)

Note: This craft is best done outdoors and in paint smocks as spattering is hard to control.

Materials: Muslin or solid color cotton fabric, measuring stick, pencil, pinking shears, wax paper, assortment of leaves, heavy books, fabric paints or liquid dyes, shallow, disposable containers for paint or dye, old toothbrushes, craft sticks, newspapers, paint smocks. Optional—scissors, sewing machine and thread, straight pins, sponges.

Preparation: Wash and dry fabric to preshrink. Use pinking shears to cut fabric into 20-inch (50-cm) squares—one for each child. (Using pinking shears will finish edges of fabric. Optional: Use regular scissors to cut fabric and finish edges by turning under and stitching on a sewing machine.) Gather various sizes and shapes of leaves. Place under heavy book overnight to flatten. Cover work area with newspapers. Pour small amounts of paint or dye in pans.

Instruct each child in the following procedures:
- Place sheets of wax paper over newspapers and lay fabric square on top.
- Select leaves and arrange them on fabric square.
- Dip toothbrush into paint and shake off excess.
- Holding the toothbrush over a leaf, rub the craft stick across the bristles of the brush. The paint will spatter on the leaf and fabric. Spatter entire surface of fabric. Repeat, using another color of paint.
- When paint is dry, remove leaves.
- Fold fabric in half diagonally and tie around neck (see sketch).

Enrichment Idea: Pin leaves to fabric to secure. Dip damp sponges in paint and dab around edges of leaves. Remove leaves from fabric and sponge a contrasting color of paint inside leaf forms.

Outdoor Life: Have you ever wondered why trees have leaves? Leaves help trees get energy from the sun so they can grow. Many trees drop their leaves during the fall and grow new leaves in the spring.

Finger Puppets

(ONE-DAY PROJECT/30 MINUTES)

Materials: Finger Puppet Patterns, white card stock paper, crayons, scissors, photocopier.

Preparation: Photocopy Finger Puppet Patterns onto card stock—one set for each child. Cut out finger holes where indicated.

Instruct each child in the following procedures:
- Cut out the animal figures.
- Color the figures.
- Slip fingers through the holes.

Outdoor Life: Do you like climbing on rocks? Can you name some animals that climb on rocks? Bighorn sheep live in high mountain areas. They are especially good at climbing in steep, rocky areas and can jump gracefully from rock to rock without falling.

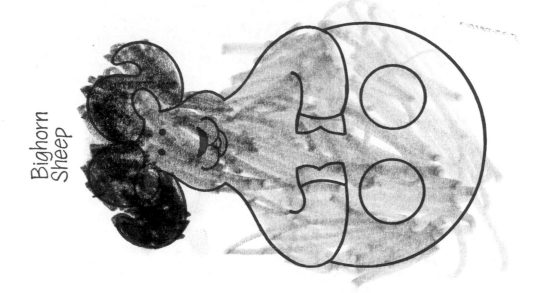

Bighorn
Sheep

Finger Puppet Patterns

Beaver

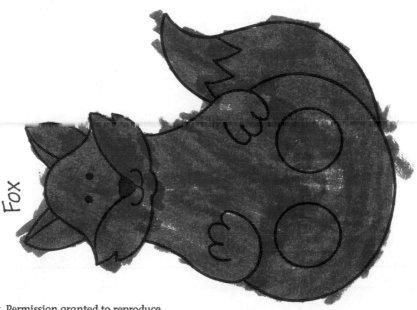

Fox

Bear Paw Stilts

(ONE- OR TWO-DAY PROJECT/60 MINUTES)

Note: Children should play with Bear Paw Stilts on a flat, grassy outdoor area or a rug-covered indoor area where there is plenty of room to move around without bumping into one another.

Materials: Bear Paw Patterns, brown paper grocery bags, photocopier, white card stock paper, ¼-inch (.6-cm) cotton cord or rope, Phillips screwdriver, hammer, pencil, scissors, tacky glue, measuring stick. For each child—two 1-pound coffee cans. Optional: To make shorter Bear Claw Stilts for younger children, use large tuna cans instead of coffee cans.

Preparation: Cut grocery bags into 2x14-inch (5x35-cm) strips—six for each child. Photocopy the Bear Paw Patterns onto white card stock paper—one set for each child. Cut cord or rope into 6-foot (1.8-m) lengths—two for each child. Use hammer and screwdriver to make two ¼-inch (.6-cm) holes directly across from each other in the bottom of each coffee can (sketch a).

Instruct each child in the following procedures:

- Cut out Bear Paws. Cut on slash lines as indicated.
- Bend paws on dotted fold lines. Center paws between holes on tops of cans and glue about 1 inch (2.5 cm) from bottom of can (sketch b).
- Make cuts in brown paper strips to make fur (sketch c).
- Cut fur strips to fit paws and glue on.
- Layer and glue remaining fur strips to cover entire surface of each can (sketch d).
- Poke the ends of the cord through holes in can. With teacher's help, tie ends together securely. (You may want to adjust the length of the cord according to height of child. Child should be able to grasp the cord with little slack when he or she is standing upright on cans and hands are at sides.)
- Step up on the cans, grab the ropes, and walk around on your Bear Paw Stilts!

Simplification Idea: Cover cans and paws with paper bag or plain paper. Children paint or color bag to make fur.

Outdoor Life: Do you know why bears have claws? Bears use their long claws to help them catch fish and pick berries to eat. They sharpen their claws by scratching on the bark of trees.

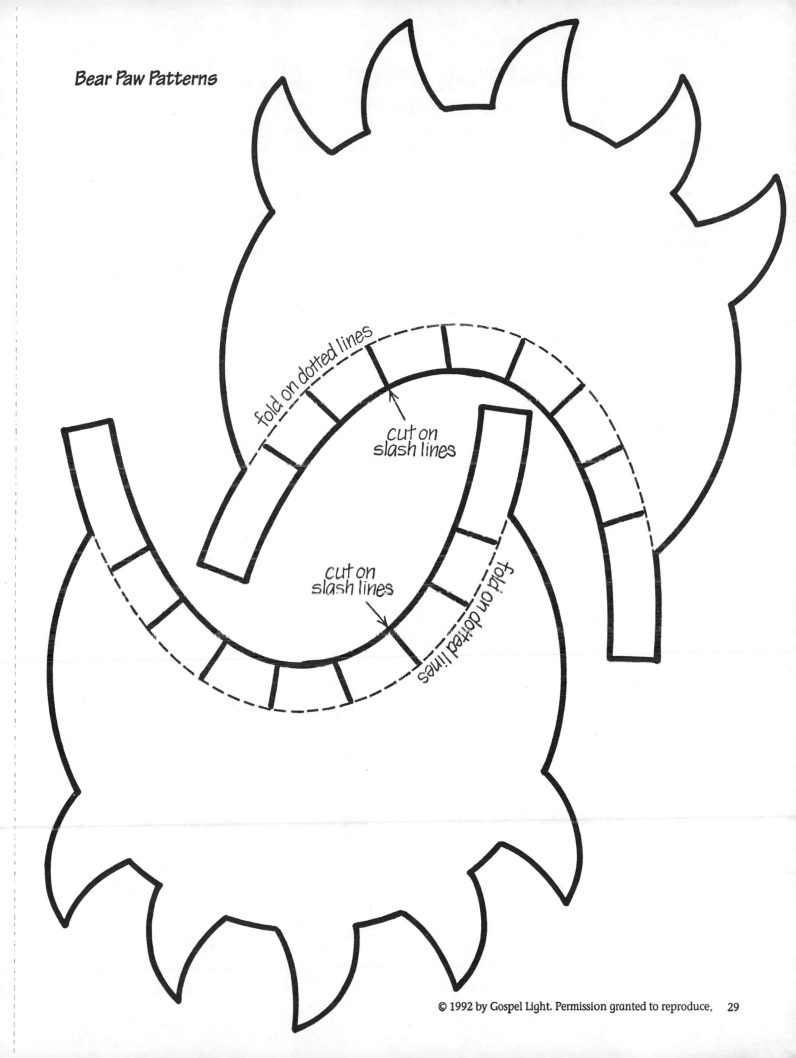

Bear Paw Patterns

fold on dotted lines

cut on
slash lines

cut on
slash lines

fold on dotted lines

29

Owl with Revolving Eyes

(ONE-DAY PROJECT/30 MINUTES)

Materials: Owl Body, Eye Disc and Beak Patterns, white card stock paper, glue, scissors, crayons or felt pens, photocopier. For each child—one ¾-inch (1.9-cm) paper fastener (brad).

Preparation: Photocopy Owl, Eye Disc and Beak Patterns onto white card stock—one set for each child. Cut out eye holes on each Owl.

Instruct each child in the following procedures:
• Cut out Owl Body, Eye Disc and Beak.
• Color Owl and Beak.
• Place Eye Disc behind Owl's head. Push paper fastener through Owl head and Eye Disc at marked points (sketch a). Open prongs of fastener to secure.
• Glue Beak to Owl head so it covers paper fastener (sketch b).
• Turn Eye Disc to make Owl's eyes revolve.

Enrichment Idea: Children glue feathers or brown paper triangles to owl's chest.

Outdoor Life: Where do you think we got the phrase "wise old owl?" Owls are called wise because they have a solemn, knowing look. Owls have very big eyes and see well at night. This comes in handy because many owls sleep during the day and stay awake at night.

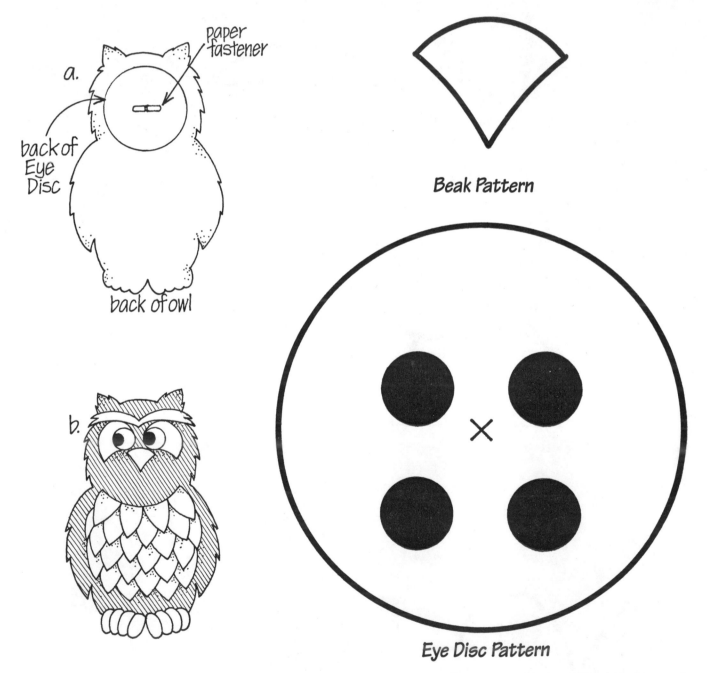

Beak Pattern

Eye Disc Pattern

cut out

cut out

Owl Pattern

Pressed Flower Sun Catcher

(ONE-DAY PROJECT/30 MINUTES)

Materials: Clear, self-adhesive paper, ruler, pencil, scissors, assortment of small pressed flowers and leaves (see "Drying and Pressing Leaves and Flowers," p. 8), straight pins, glue, yarn, heavy books. For each child—eight tongue depressors.

Preparation: Cut self-adhesive paper into 5-inch (12.5-cm) squares—two for each child. Cut yarn into 3-inch (7.5-cm) lengths—one for each child.

Instruct each child in the following procedures:

- Glue four tongue depressors in frame pattern (sketch a). Repeat with additional four depressors. Let dry.
- With teacher's help, peel paper backing from one self-adhesive square. Lay paper on table with sticky side up.
- Choose pressed flowers and leaves and arrange on sticky side of square.
- With teacher's help, peel backing from second square and lay on top of first square, sticky sides together. (Best results are achieved by beginning at one corner and working diagonally to press out air.) Remove air pockets by puncturing with a pin and pressing flat.
- Spread a thin line of glue around edges of flower square and press against tongue-depressor frame (sketch b).
- Glue loop of yarn at top for hanger (sketch b).
- Glue remaining tongue depressors to back of other frame, with hanger and flower square sandwiched between.
- Weight down with books and allow to dry.
- Hang Sun Catcher in a window.

Enrichment Idea: Paint frame with poster paints or letter a Bible verse around the edge.

Outdoor Life: What kinds of flowers grow near your house or apartment? Who waters them? During spring and summer, when it's warm, lots of wildflowers can be seen in the mountains. But no one waters them! Most mountain flowers are small and have long roots that go deep into the ground where they can find water left over from the winter's rain and snow.

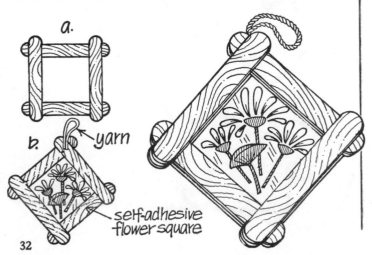

Rock Campfire Scene

(TWO-DAY PROJECT/60 MINUTES)

Materials: Tree Patterns, rocks and pebbles, twigs, acrylic paints, small paintbrushes, shallow containers for paint, construction paper, scissors, glue, newspapers, black permanent felt pens, photocopier. For each child—one shoe box.

Preparation: Photocopy Tree Patterns onto green construction paper—two trees for each child. Wash and dry rocks and pebbles, if necessary, and allow to dry. Cover work area with newspapers. Pour paint into containers.

Instruct each child in the following procedures:

DAY ONE:
- Choose several rocks and paint faces and clothes on them to make "campers." Let dry.
- Cut mountain shape from construction paper and glue to back of shoe box.
- Cut out Tree Patterns. Fold flaps back along dotted lines (sketch a). Fold trees in half to crease and then open partially. Squeeze a line of glue along underside of each flap and glue trees in place where desired.

DAY TWO:
- Use felt pen to draw details on rock people and box background.
- Glue pebbles and twigs to bottom of shoe box to form campfire (sketch b).
- Place rock campers around campfire. (Children can play with campfire scene by moving rock campers around.)

Outdoor Life: Have you ever gone camping? What do you like to do when you go camping? Some people like going to the mountains so they can enjoy the things that God has created like trees, flowers, streams and fresh air.

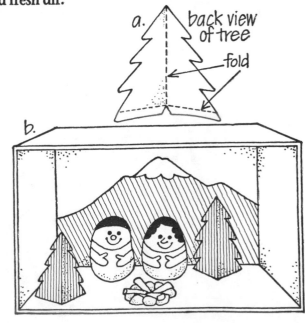

Tree Patterns

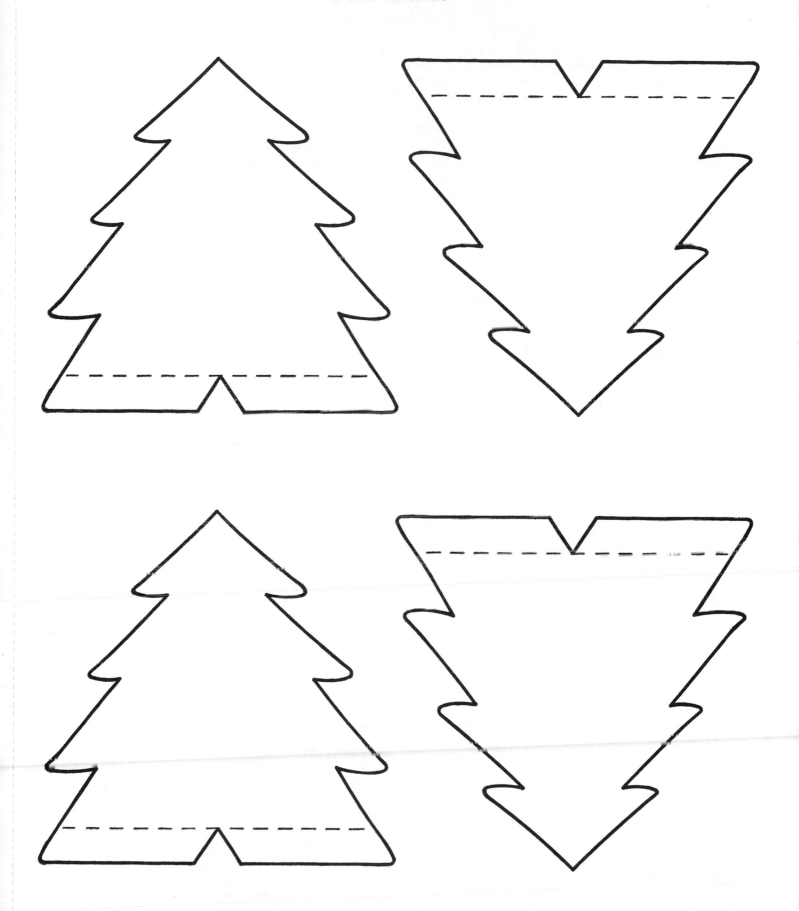

33

Pinecone Rabbit
(ONE-DAY PROJECT/30 MINUTES)

Materials: Tacky glue, brightly-colored poster board, scissors, ruler, pencil, straw flowers, air-drying clay. For each child—two oblong seed pods, six pussy willow blossoms or small white pom-poms, two pinecones (one pinecone should be smaller than the other).

Preparation: Cut poster board into 3-inch (7.5-cm) squares—one for each child.

Instruct each child in the following procedures:

• Squeeze a drop of glue in center of poster-board base.
• Roll small piece of clay into a ball and press down on top of glue.
• Squeeze a drop of glue on clay, then press the base of the larger pinecone onto clay.
• Squeeze several drops of glue onto top of pinecone and place a small lump of clay on top of glue.
• Squeeze a drop of glue on top of clay and press smaller pinecone onto the clay at a 45 degree angle (sketch a).
• To make paws, glue two pussy willow blossoms to poster board at base of body and two to petals near center of body (sketch b).
• To make tail, glue one pussy willow blossom on the lower back of pinecone body.
• To make ears, glue seed pods in slots between scales on pinecone head.
• Glue two straw flower blossoms to pinecone head for eyes. Glue a pussy willow blossom to head for nose.
• For whiskers, break dried flower stems into pieces and glue between petals on head. Let dry.

Outdoor Life: Arrange to have one or more pet rabbits brought in to your classroom. Allow children to observe the rabbits and hold them. **A type of rabbit called the mountain hare lives in mountain areas. During the summer the mountain hare has a gray-brown coat of fur. As winter approaches, the rabbit's fur turns white like the winter snow. This makes it hard for attackers to see it.**

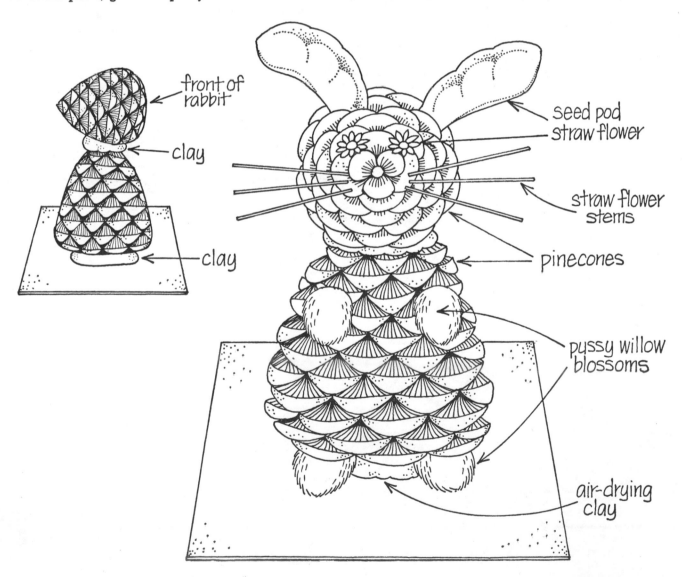

front of rabbit

clay

clay

seed pod
straw flower

straw flower stems

pinecones

pussy willow blossoms

air-drying clay

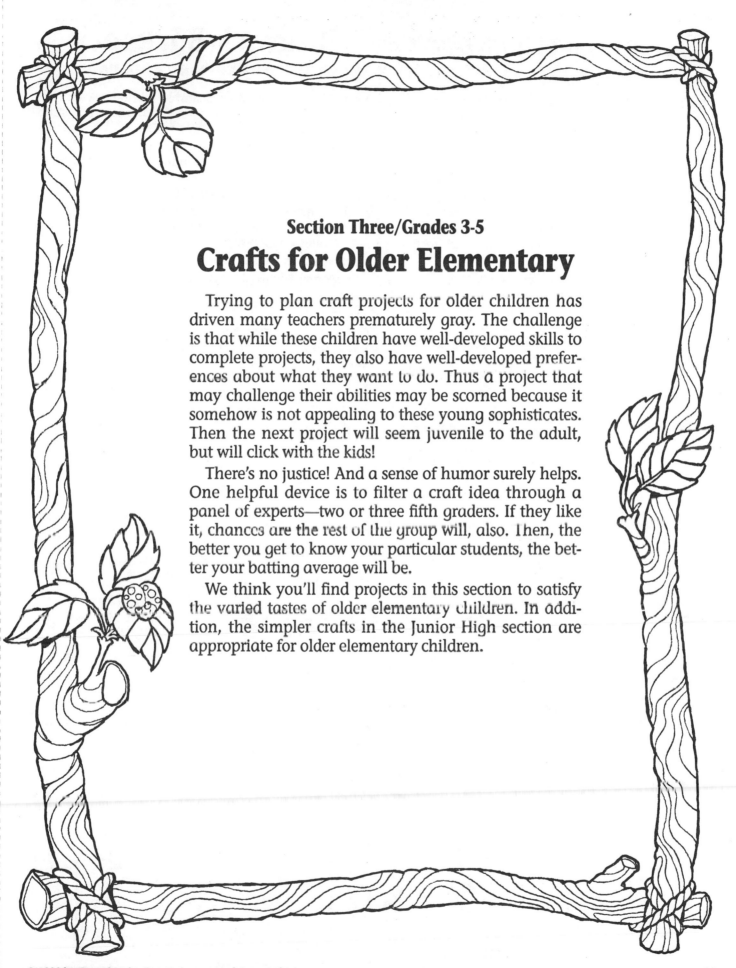

Section Three/Grades 3-5
Crafts for Older Elementary

Trying to plan craft projects for older children has driven many teachers prematurely gray. The challenge is that while these children have well-developed skills to complete projects, they also have well-developed preferences about what they want to do. Thus a project that may challenge their abilities may be scorned because it somehow is not appealing to these young sophisticates. Then the next project will seem juvenile to the adult, but will click with the kids!

There's no justice! And a sense of humor surely helps. One helpful device is to filter a craft idea through a panel of experts—two or three fifth graders. If they like it, chances are the rest of the group will, also. Then, the better you get to know your particular students, the better your batting average will be.

We think you'll find projects in this section to satisfy the varied tastes of older elementary children. In addition, the simpler crafts in the Junior High section are appropriate for older elementary children.

Tic-Tac-Toe Backpack
(ONE-DAY PROJECT/30 MINUTES)

Note: This craft requires a simple fabric backpack for each student. For backpack materials and sewing instructions see page 7.

Materials: Various colors of rickrack and ribbon, Fabric Tac (or other washable adhesive for fabric crafts), Velcro, scissors, rulers. For each student—five large, flat buttons of one color; four large, flat buttons of another color; one backpack.

Preparation: Leaving top and bottom strips attached, cut Velcro into ½-inch (1.25-cm) pieces—nine for each student.

Instruct each student in the following procedures:
- Measure and cut rickrack or ribbon into four 10-inch (25-cm) lengths. (Cut four additional lengths of contrasting colors if layered effect is desired.)
- Use Fabric Tac to glue rickrack or ribbon onto front of backpack to form tic-tac-toe grid.
- Separate Velcro pieces. Glue stiff pieces to centers of squares on the tic-tac-toe grid (sketch a).
- Glue soft Velcro pieces onto the backs of buttons (sketch b).
- Allow to dry at least 20 minutes before playing game.

Outdoor Life: When will you use your backpack? Backpacks are a handy way to carry things while you're walking or riding your bike. When you walk or ride a bike instead of riding in a car, you are cutting down on air pollution and helping make the earth a cleaner, healthier place to be. What are some other ways you can help cut down on pollution?

Rickrack Backpack
(ONE- OR TWO-DAY PROJECT/60 MINUTES)

Note: This craft requires a simple fabric backpack for each student. For backpack materials and sewing instructions see page 7.

Materials: Scissors, pencils, scratch paper, Fabric Tac (or other washable adhesive for fabric crafts), various colors and sizes of cord, ribbon, rickrack, buttons, sequins and plastic jewels. For each student—one backpack.

Instruct each student in the following procedures:
- Use pencil to draw design ideas on paper. (Large, simple outlines work best.)
- On backpack, pencil outline of final design choice.
- Use Fabric Tac to glue rickrack, ribbon or cord on outline.
- Glue on additional items to complete design.

Outdoor Life: Cars are one of the biggest causes of air pollution in the world. What is a way you might help cut down on air pollution? Next time you need to go somewhere, think about grabbing your backpack and hopping on your bike or walking, instead of asking for a ride. You can help keep the earth a wonderful, clean place to be!

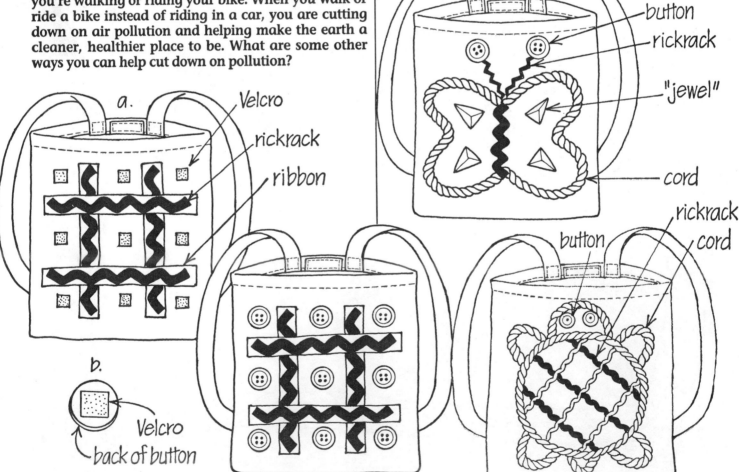

Flowering Tiles

(ONE-DAY PROJECT/30 MINUTES)

Materials: Glue, Polymer medium or thinned white glue in shallow containers, sponge brushes, clear acrylic spray, scissors, assortment of pressed flowers and leaves (see "Drying and Pressing Leaves and Flowers," p. 8), ½-inch (1.25-cm) wide adhesive-backed magnetic strip, heavy books, newspapers. For each student—two solid-color, 3-inch (7.5-cm) tiles.

Preparation: Cut magnetic strip into 2½-inch (6.25-cm) lengths—four for each student. Squeeze two lines of glue on the back of each tile and apply two adhesive strips (sketch a). Weight tiles down with heavy books while glue dries overnight. Cover work area with newspapers.

Instruct each student in the following procedures:
- Arrange flowers and leaves on tiles.
- Remove the flower arrangement and brush a coat of Polymer or thinned glue over the tile surface (sketch b).
- While surface is wet, place flowers carefully, one by one, on the tile. Tap down each petal and leaf with brush handle. (Try not to touch the flowers with your fingers. Any glue on your fingers will cause the flowers to stick to them and tear.)
- Allow first tile to dry while you work on another.
- When tile is dry, dip brush into Polymer or thinned glue and carefully dab brush over flowers to form a protective coating. Allow to dry.
- Spray tiles with acrylic spray.

Enrichment Ideas: Use larger tiles and back with picture hangers to make wall hangings. Check out books on wildflowers from the library. Students identify flowers they used for their projects.

Outdoor Life: What kinds of flowers grow near your home? Flowers that grow in mountains and meadows are called wildflowers. They are called wild because no person plants them or takes care of them.

Nature Image Plaque

(TWO-DAY PROJECT/30 MINUTES EACH DAY)

Materials: Earth tone air-drying clay, rolling pins, newspapers, an assortment of fresh leaves, weeds and flowers, other nature items such as small pinecones, pebbles and seed pods; blunt table knives, pencils, watercolor paints and paintbrushes, containers for water. For each student: 6-inch (15-cm) strip of rawhide lacing. (Note: Watercolor dyes provide more intense colors than standard watercolor paint. They are available at graphic art supply stores.)

Preparation: Cover work area with newspapers.

Instruct each student in the following procedures:

DAY ONE:
- Roll a lump of clay into ³⁄₈-inch (.9-cm) thickness.
- Use knife to cut clay into desired shape.
- Select nature items and arrange on clay.
- Carefully press nature items into wet clay to make impressions and then remove.
- Use pencil to punch a hole at top of plaque for hanger.
- Repeat entire process to make additional plaques as time allows.
- Allow to dry overnight.

DAY TWO:
- Enhance nature item impressions by painting with watercolors.
- Thread rawhide strip through hole and tie knot for hanger.

Outdoor Life: Have you ever seen wildflowers growing high in the mountains? Although the weather is often very cold at high altitudes, some of the world's most beautiful flowers grow at heights of almost ten thousand feet! Wildflowers can even grow among the rocks above a mountain's tree line. The long roots search out unfrozen water deep below. Certain varieties of alpine flowers, such as edelweiss, have a fuzzy hair-like covering that keeps warmth and moisture in.

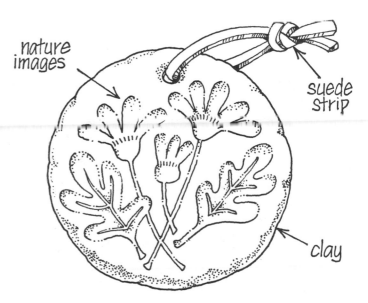

Pop-Up Frog
(ONE-DAY PROJECT/30 MINUTES)

Materials: Frog Body and Frog Eye Patterns, bright pink lightweight poster board, bright green and yellow card stock or construction paper, round ring-binder reinforcements, pencils, felt pens, ruler, glue, scissors, photocopier. For each student—two 20mm wiggle eyes.

Preparation: Photocopy Frog Body and Frog Eye Pattern onto bright green card stock or construction paper—one for each student. Cut pink poster board into 81/2x11-inch (21.25x27.5-cm) rectangles—one for each student. Cut yellow paper into 4-inch (10-cm) squares—one for each student.

Instruct each student in the following procedures:
- Cut out Frog Body and Frog Eye Patterns. Trace Eye Pattern onto yellow paper square twice and cut out.
- Fold frog in half and cut along mouth opening. Fold along mouth fold lines to crease (sketch a).
- Unfold frog, placing photocopied side down. Fold eye and leg areas toward you. Push mouth to pop out toward you (sketch b). Center fold of frog folds away from you.
- Spread glue on back side of eye and leg areas.
- Fold pink poster board rectangle in half. Press center of Frog Body into fold of poster board and push down. Allow to dry.
- Glue eyelids to Frog Body. Glue wiggle eyes to eyelids.
- Decorate Frog Body with round ring-binder reinforcements. Use felt pens to color reinforcements.

Enrichment Ideas: Use Pop-Up Frog as a card or invitation to a special event. Write a message on the outside or inside of pink poster board.

Outdoor Life: Arrange to have in your classroom one or more frogs which students can observe and hold.

There are many different kinds of frogs. Can you guess how the leopard frog got its name? (It has leopard-like spots.) The life of a leopard frog begins when a tadpole is hatched. The tiny tadpole is born and lives like a fish underwater. Slowly the tadpole develops into a frog which lives on land in moist, grassy meadows.

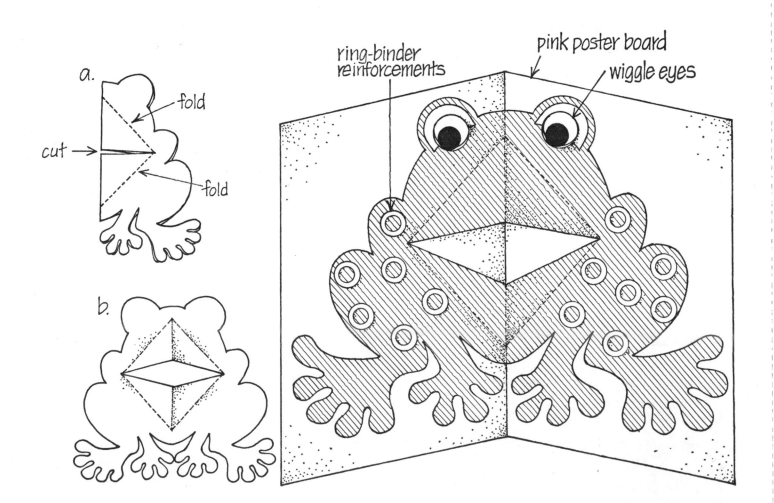

a. fold / cut / fold

b.

ring-binder reinforcements   pink poster board   wiggle eyes

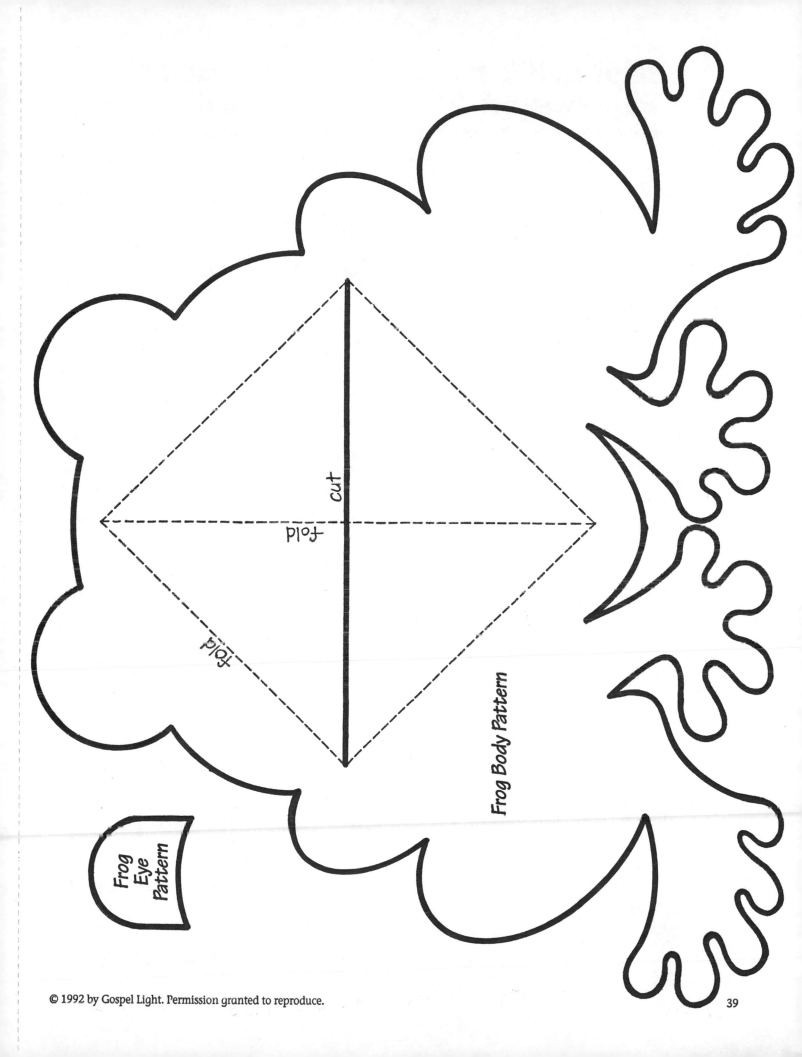

cut

fold

fold

Frog Body Pattern

Frog
Eye
Pattern

Helpless Hiker Paperweight

(ONE-DAY PROJECT/30 MINUTES)

Materials: Twigs, acorns, brightly-colored card stock or construction paper, scissors, felt pens, tape, tacky glue. For each student—a fist-sized rock with one flat side and several extra rocks to use as reinforcements while glue dries.

Preparation: Wash rocks, if necessary, and allow to dry.

Instruct each student in the following procedures:

• Break two twigs to desired length for legs.

• Glue legs to bottom of rock.

• Glue acorns to the ends of twigs for feet. (Use extra rocks to prop up acorns while drying.)

• Cut a rectangle from card stock or construction paper. Letter the word "Help!" on the paper.

• Glue paper to a twig to make sign. Secure with tape.

• Glue sign to back side of rock. (Use extra rocks to prop up sign while drying.)

Enrichment Idea: Students create their own messages for signs.

Outdoor Life: Have you ever gone hiking or backpacking in the mountains? People have always been attracted to the mountains. Since the earliest times, daring climbers have tried to scale the highest peaks. Whenever we're hiking in the mountains it's important to be with an adult and be careful!

Forest Animal Mobile

(ONE-DAY PROJECT/30 MINUTES)

Materials: Animal Head Patterns, white paper, string, glue, scissors, ruler, crayons or felt pens, photocopier. For each student—one tree branch at least 16 inches (40 cm) long.

Preparation: Photocopy Animal Head Patterns onto paper—two copies for each student. Cut string into 10-inch (25-cm) lengths—eight for each student.

Instruct each student in the following procedures:

• Color two of each animal head and cut out.

• Glue like animal heads together, inserting length of string between the two heads.

• Attach animal heads to mobile by tying ends of string to branch.

• Tie remaining three pieces of string near the center branch and knot at top to form hanger.

Enrichment Ideas: Hang nature items such as acorns or small pinecones between animal heads. Students letter names of animals on white paper and hang below heads.

Outdoor Life: What is your favorite mountain animal? How would you feel if you found out your favorite animal had become extinct? The brown bear is an endangered species. The largest bear in the world, it can grow to be nine feet long and weigh over 1,500 pounds. The brown bear needs a large area of land where it can live and search for food. Because people keep taking the land where brown bears live, many bears are dying and soon there may be none left at all. Some zoos have special programs to help endangered species like the brown bear.

40

Beaver

Raccoon

Owl

Moose

Bear

41

Mountain View Diorama

The following pages contain instructions for making a Mountain View Diorama. This project will take from two to five days to complete depending on the options you choose. Make a sample diorama ahead of time. Have your students begin by making the Background Scene. Then choose one or more of the other options, depending on the time and materials available, to complete the Diorama.

Enrichment Idea: Before beginning project, students draw design ideas on paper.

Outdoor Life: What do you like to do in the mountains? Some people enjoy exciting sports like rock climbing, river rafting, skiing and backpacking. Others enjoy playing in creeks, hiking or sitting quietly on a rock while painting, drawing or writing poems about what they see.

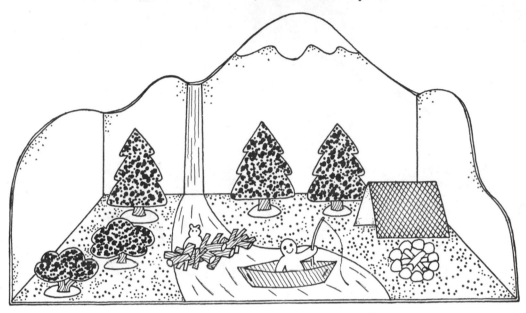

Mountain View Diorama—Background Scene

(ONE-DAY PROJECT/30 MINUTES)

Materials: Craft knife, scissors, pencils, tempera paints, shallow containers for paint, paintbrushes, newspapers. For each student—one cardboard box, approximately 9×12×18 inches (22.5×30×45 cm).

Preparation: Use craft knife to cut off top flaps and front of each box. Pour paint into containers. Cover work area with newspapers.

Instruct each student in the following procedures:

- Draw the outline of a mountain range on the sides and back of your box. Use scissors to cut out. (Teacher may need to use craft knife to cut along outline.)
- Lightly sketch details onto background scene, including a river coming down from the mountains. Then paint mountains and river. Paint remaining area green or brown for ground. Let dry.

Outdoor Life: Before students begin project, ask them to imagine a mountain scene. This will give each individual ideas from which to work. **Close your eyes and imagine you are in the mountains. What do you see? What colors do you see? Is it morning, afternoon or evening? What color is the sky?**

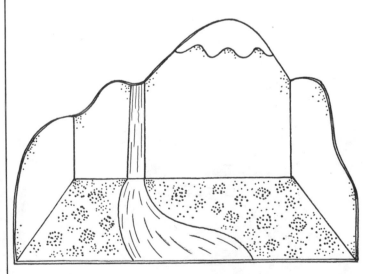

Mountain View Diorama— Trees and Shrubs

(ONE-DAY PROJECT/30 MINUTES)

Materials: Air-drying clay, twigs, heavy white art paper, several shades of green tempera paint, sponges, shallow containers, scissors, glue, tape, newspapers.

Preparation: Pour paint into shallow containers. Cut sponges into 2-inch (5-cm) squares. Cover work area with newspapers.

Instruct each student in the following procedures:

• Sponge paint various shades of green onto art paper (sketch a). Let dry.

• Cut tree and shrub shapes from painted paper.

• Glue twigs to back of tree and shrub shapes and secure with tape (sketch b).

• Use clay to form bases for trees. Press twig ends into clay bases. Let dry.

• Glue tree bases in place, being careful to plan for further additions to diorama.

Outdoor Life: A tree is a plant like a shrub or a flower. However, trees are stronger, bigger and live longer than any other kind of plant. Trees are not only beautiful to look at, they provide shade and they produce clean air for us to breathe.

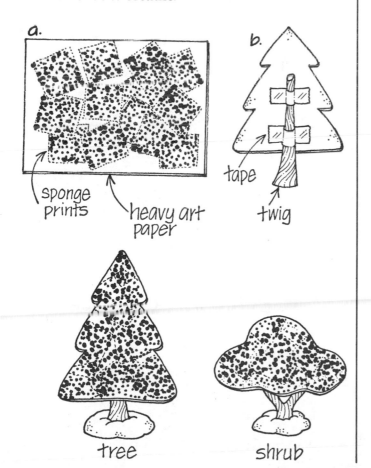

a. sponge prints / heavy art paper

b. tape / twig

tree   shrub

Mountain View Diorama— Tent and Campfire

(ONE-DAY PROJECT/30 MINUTES)

Materials: Twigs, pebbles, bright solid-colored fabric, felt pens, scissors, glue. For each student—one small index card.

Instruct each student in the following procedures:

• Trace around index card onto burlap fabric and cut out.

• Glue fabric to index card. Let dry.

• Arrange pebbles and twigs to form campfire. Glue in place.

• Fold fabric-covered card in half to form tent. Glue in place.

Outdoor Life: Groups of people like to go camping so they can enjoy nature and have a good time with their friends. What is your favorite thing about camping? What is your least favorite thing about camping?

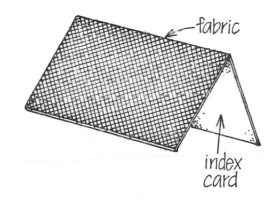

fabric / index card

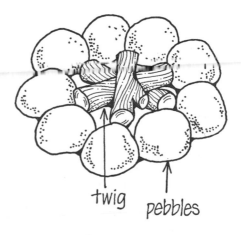

twig   pebbles

Mountain View Diorama— Beaver and Beaver Dam

(ONE-DAY PROJECT/30 MINUTES)

Materials: Twigs, earth tone air-drying clay, glue.

Instruct each student in the following procedures:

• Use clay to form beaver. Let dry.
• Use twigs to assemble beaver dam across river. Glue in place.
• Glue beaver in place.

Outdoor Life: What is something you'd like to be known for—something you'd like to be able to do really well? Beavers are known for their hard work at building dams. They use their sharp teeth to cut down trees. After cutting the trees into manageable lengths, the beaver carries the logs to a stream where they are used along with mud and rocks to build a dam. The dam then creates a pond where the beaver will build its home.

clay beaver

twigs glued to "river"

Mountain View Diorama— Fisherman and Canoe

(ONE-DAY PROJECT/30 MINUTES)

Materials: Canoe Pattern, construction paper, scissors, earth tone air-drying clay, string, twigs, stapler and staples, glue, photocopier.

Preparation: Photocopy Canoe Pattern onto construction paper—one for each student.

Instruct each student in the following procedures:

• Cut out canoe shape. Fold on fold lines and staple (sketch a).
• Use clay to form a fisherman. Attach a twig to fisherman's arm for fishing pole. Tie string to twig for fishing line (sketch b). Let dry.
• Glue canoe in place on river (sketch c).
• Glue fisherman in place inside canoe.

Outdoor Life: What kinds of boats have you ridden in? People have been making and using canoes for thousands of years. Native Americans were experts at making canoes and used them as a main source of transportation. Now people enjoy paddling canoes for fun, when they are visiting mountain rivers and lakes.

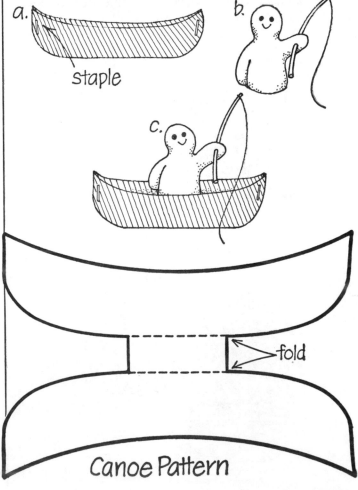

a.

staple

b.

c.

fold

Canoe Pattern

Tree Branch Frame

(ONE- OR TWO-DAY PROJECT/60 MINUTES)

Materials: Small tree branches 1/4-1/2-inch (.6-.1.25-cm) in diameter, saw, sandpaper, 1/8-inch (.3-cm) suede or leather strips, scissors, rulers, glue, cardboard, pencils, camera, film. For each student—one picture hanger. Optional: Discarded nature magazines and calendars.

Preparation: Take a snapshot of each student in advance and have photos developed. Optional: Students cut nature pictures from magazines to put in their frames. Cut suede strips into 5-inch (12.5-cm) lengths—four for each student.

Instruct each student in the following procedures:
- Trace around photo onto cardboard and cut out.
- Measure the sides of cardboard. Choose tree branches and break or saw into eight lengths—two branches corresponding to each of the four sides of the cardboard (sketch a). Each branch should be 2 inches (5 cm) longer than the corresponding side of cardboard.
- Use sandpaper to sand branch ends and rough spots.
- Lay horizontal branches under cardboard (sketch b).
- Lay vertical branches on top of horizontal branches, next to cardboard (sketch c).
- Carefully lift cardboard off branches. Have a partner hold branches in place as you tie a suede strip at each corner of frame to secure branches (sketch d). Suede will form an "X" on each corner of the front side of the frame (sketch e).
- Glue photo to cardboard.
- Squeeze a line of glue along horizontal branches.
- Lay photo facedown on frame. Let dry.
- Attach picture hanger to cardboard.

Outdoor Life: What is the largest plant you have ever seen? A tree is stronger, bigger and lives longer than any other kind of plant. Trees are perennial, which means they don't die at the end of every summer like many other plants. Instead, they live on from year to year. Sometimes trees live for hundreds of years. Oak trees, for example, can live between 500 to 800 years! Redwoods can keep growing for thousands of years. Some huge trees which are alive today were just starting to grow when Jesus was alive—2,000 years ago!

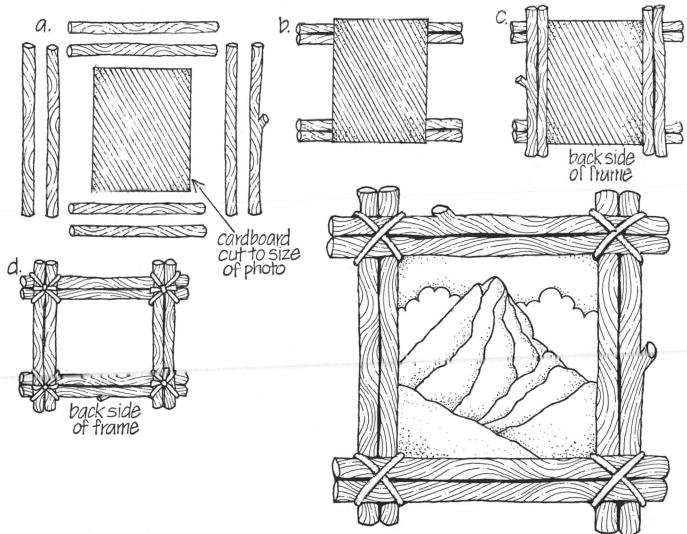

a.

b.

c. back side of frame

cardboard cut to size of photo

d. back side of frame

Secret Stone

(TWO-DAY PROJECT/30 MINUTES EACH DAY)

Materials: Newspaper, scissors, aluminum foil, ruler, flour, water, bowl, spoon, shallow containers, old tooth-brushes, craft sticks, paintbrushes, several large cardboard boxes, craft knife, black and white acrylic paint, clear acrylic spray, paper plates, paint shirts. For each student—one baby food jar.

Preparation: For Day One: Cut some newspaper into strips 1-inch (2.5-cm) wide and of varying lengths. Leave some newspaper uncut. To make papier-mâché mixture: Combine one part flour to two parts water and mix until smooth. Pour mixture into shallow containers. Tear foil into 6-inch (15-cm) lengths. For Day Two: Combine some of the white and black paint to make gray. Reserve some white and black paint for spattering. Pour paint into shallow containers. (Note: Depending on the consistency of the paint, you may need to add a small amount of water in order to get a fine spray when spattering. Be careful not to over-dilute the paint or the spatters will run.) Make spattering stations out of large cardboard boxes by cutting out a large "window" in the side of each box (sketch a). Set boxes outside if possible. Cover work areas with newspaper.

Instruct each student in the following procedures:
DAY ONE:
- Place jar upside down in front of you with the lid on.
- Dip a newspaper strip into papier-mâché mixture. Pull strip between fingers to remove excess mixture. Wrap strip around the jar. Continue adding strips until jar is covered. (Do not cover the lid.)
- Crumple foil into a long coil and wrap around jar lid, pinching the ends together to keep it in place (sketch b). This will create space between the papier-mâché and the jar so it will be possible to unscrew jar lid.

- Tear off several pieces of newspaper large enough to cover your jar. Crumple newspaper, dip in papier-mâché mixture and attach to jar, building up the form of a rock (sketch c). Make the rock shape irregular to give it a realistic appearance.
- Cover the rock shape with more newspaper strips dipped in the papier-mâché mixture. Press and smooth down the strips. (Cover the ring of foil around the jar lid, but don't cover the lid.)
- Allow to dry overnight.

DAY TWO:
- Remove the ring of foil around the lid.
- Place rock on a paper plate.
- Paint rock completely with gray paint.
- Place plate and rock inside box at a spattering station.
- Dip a toothbrush in the black paint. Holding the toothbrush bristle-side down, a few inches away from the rock, run craft stick along the bristles, allowing the paint to lightly spray and spatter rock.
- Repeat spattering process using white paint. Let dry.
- Spray with clear acrylic spray. Let dry.
- Students use rock as a hiding place for small items.

Enrichment Idea: Students spatter additional colors on their rocks.

Outdoor Life: **Did you know the earth is made up of many different kinds of rocks? In some places the rocks are arranged in layers. These rock layers are like pages in a book. Geologists learn to read them to find out about changes in climate, ancient lava flows and changes in land and sea. Fossils embedded in the layers of rock may tell geologists about plants and animals that lived a long time ago.**

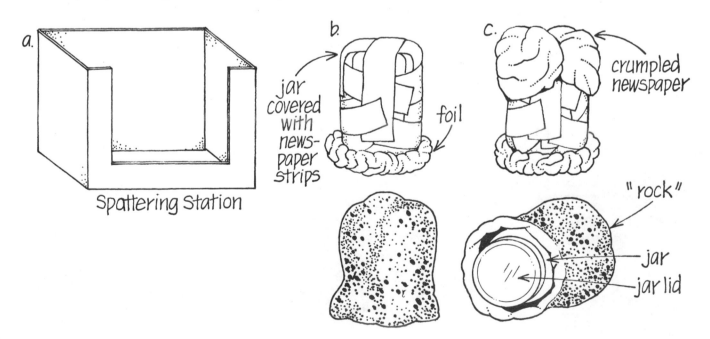

a. Spattering Station

b. jar covered with newspaper strips / foil

c. crumpled newspaper

"rock" / jar / jar lid

Leaf-Covered Box

(TWO-DAY PROJECT/30 MINUTES EACH DAY)

Materials: Polymer medium (water-based varnish available at craft supply stores) or thinned white glue, shallow containers, paintbrushes, craft knives, wax paper, newspapers, irons, ironing boards, assortment of fresh (flexible, not brittle) leaves, warm soapy water for clean-up. For each student—one cardboard pencil box (available where school supplies are sold).

Preparation: Pour polymer or glue into shallow containers. Cover work area with newspapers. Set up iron and ironing boards away from area where students will be working.

Instruct each student in the following procedures:

DAY ONE:

- Place leaves between two sheets of wax paper and top with a sheet of newspaper. Press gently with a warm iron to coat leaves with wax.
- Brush box top and sides with a coat of polymer. Allow to dry.
- Remove leaves from wax paper. Paint the underside of each leaf with polymer. This coating will give the leaves more flexibility and make them easier to handle.
- Brush a second coat of polymer onto box.
- Lay leaves on the wet surface, overlapping to cover top and sides of box. Leaves should lie over opening of box (sketch a). Try not to get any polymer on the top side of leaves.
- As you complete each section of the box, place a sheet of wax paper on the surface, then cover wax paper with a sheet of newspaper and press gently with a warm iron. (Do not move iron back and forth.) This will help the leaves to adhere. Pull off wax paper immediately, while it's still warm, or wax paper will stick to box and pull up leaves.
- Repeat process of painting sections with polymer, attaching leaves and ironing, until entire box is covered. Let dry.

DAY TWO:

- With craft knife, make a slit around box opening.
- Brush polymer over entire box so that all leaves are completely coated. Let dry (about 10 minutes).
- Apply one or two more coats of polymer, allowing to dry between coats.
- Use craft knife to make slit again, if necessary.

Enrichment Ideas: Use flower petals as well as leaves to cover box. Line box with felt, shelf paper or adhesive-backed covering.

Outdoor Life: Who can tell me the two main types of trees? (Needleleaf and broadleaf.)

Needleleaf trees have needle-shaped leaves and are evergreen—they keep their leaves during the winter. Broadleaf trees usually have broad flat leaves and are deciduous—their leaves fall off in autumn. New leaves grow on broadleaf trees each spring. **Which type of leaves are we using to decorate our boxes? What types of trees do you have near your house or apartment?**

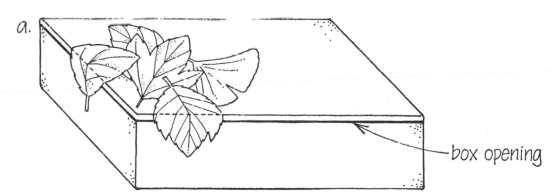

a.

box opening

Really Neat Recycling Bins

(ONE-DAY PROJECT/30 MINUTES)

Materials: Discarded magazines and calendars containing nature pictures, construction paper, glue, scissors. For each student—one cardboard packing box. Optional—clear self-adhesive paper, additional boxes.

Preparations: Find out about recycling opportunities in your area (i.e. curbside recycling, aluminum can redemption machines, glass recycling center, etc.). Be prepared to explain these opportunities to your students.

Instruct each student in the following procedures:

• Cut nature pictures from magazines.

• Glue pictures to one side of packing box.

• Decide what item you will save in your bin (aluminum, plastic, paper or glass). Cut out letters from magazines to tell what you will recycle. Glue letters to a strip of construction paper. Glue strip to box.

• Optional: Cover front of box with clear self-adhesive paper.

• Make additional Recycling Bins as time allows.

Simplification Idea: Students decorate brown grocery bags instead of packing boxes.

Outdoor Life: What do you recycle at your house? Every day people throw away more garbage and every day more of our beautiful earth is being filled with more garbage dumps and landfills. With a little effort we can reduce the amount of garbage we throw away by recycling and reusing things like glass bottles, aluminum and newspapers. Let's recycle and help keep the earth a clean and beautiful place to live.

Embossed Metal Magnets

(ONE-DAY PROJECT/30 MINUTES)

Materials: Bear, Fox and Squirrel Patterns, paper, photocopier, thin sheets of copper, brass or aluminum, ruler, glue gun and glue sticks, craft sticks, scissors, transparent tape, small, round magnets, newspapers. For each student—one crochet hook or other rounded instrument such as a ballpoint pen.

Preparation: Photocopy Patterns onto paper—one set for each student. Cut metal into 6-inch (15-cm) squares—one for each student.

Instruct each student in the following procedures:

• Choose one Animal Pattern and cut out along dotted line.

• Tape pattern to metal.

• Place metal on a stack of newspapers.

• Using a crochet hook or other rounded instrument, press hard and trace outline and features of animal.

• Remove pattern and turn metal over. Use craft stick to press down and rub against metal between outlines. This will give the animal a smooth, raised effect.

• Use scissors to cut around animal about ⅛-inch (.3-cm) beyond the outline.

• Using glue gun, attach magnet to back of animal.

Enrichment Idea: Students create their own designs for metal magnets.

Outdoor Life: Tree squirrels are proud of their graceful, showy tails. They take care to keep their tails well groomed. But the squirrel's tail is not *only* something pretty to look at. Do you know why a squirrel's tail is so important? (A tree squirrel's tail helps the squirrel keep its balance as it makes daring leaps from tree branch to tree branch.)

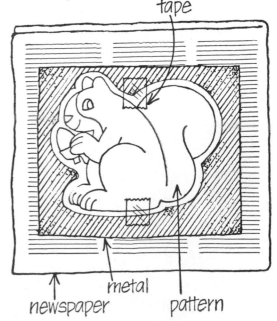

48

Fox

Bear

Squirrel

49

Pop-Up Bear Card

(ONE-DAY PROJECT/30 MINUTES)

Materials: Mountain, Trees and Bear Patterns (p. 51,52), white card-stock paper, sponges, photocopier, tempera paint in several shades of brown and green, shallow containers, scissors, newspapers, felt pens.

Preparation: Photocopy Mountain, Trees and Bear Patterns onto card stock—one set for each student. Cut damp sponges into 1-inch (2.5-cm) triangles and squares. Pour paint into shallow containers. Cover work area with newspapers.

Instruct each student in the following procedures:

- Cut out Trees and Mountain Patterns on heavy solid lines, including flap in center of mountain.
- Sponge different shades of green paint onto Trees and Mountain. Let dry.
- Cut out Bear Pattern on heavy solid lines.
- Sponge different shades of brown paint onto Bear. Let dry.
- Fold Mountain flaps on dotted lines (sketch a).
- Turn Trees facedown and glue to Mountain flap (sketch a).
- Glue Bear to Trees and Mountain at flaps (sketch b).
- On the blank space at the bottom of card students may letter greeting, invitation or poem, draw a campfire, or draw grass or dirt.
- Fold Trees up and down to make Bear "pop up."

Outdoor Life: One of the largest mountain animals is the grizzly bear. Grizzlies survive cold mountain winters by sleeping in dens, which are often buried deep under the snow. In the spring, grizzlies come out of their dens to look for food.

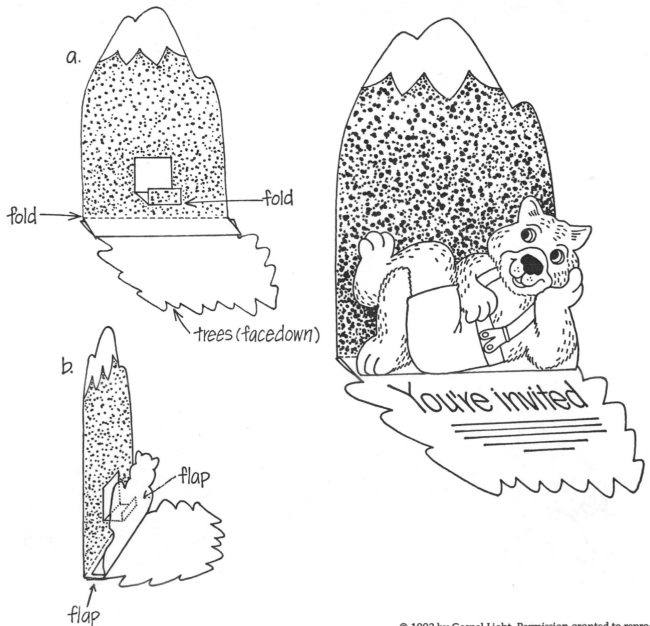

a.

fold

fold

trees (facedown)

b.

flap

flap

You're invited

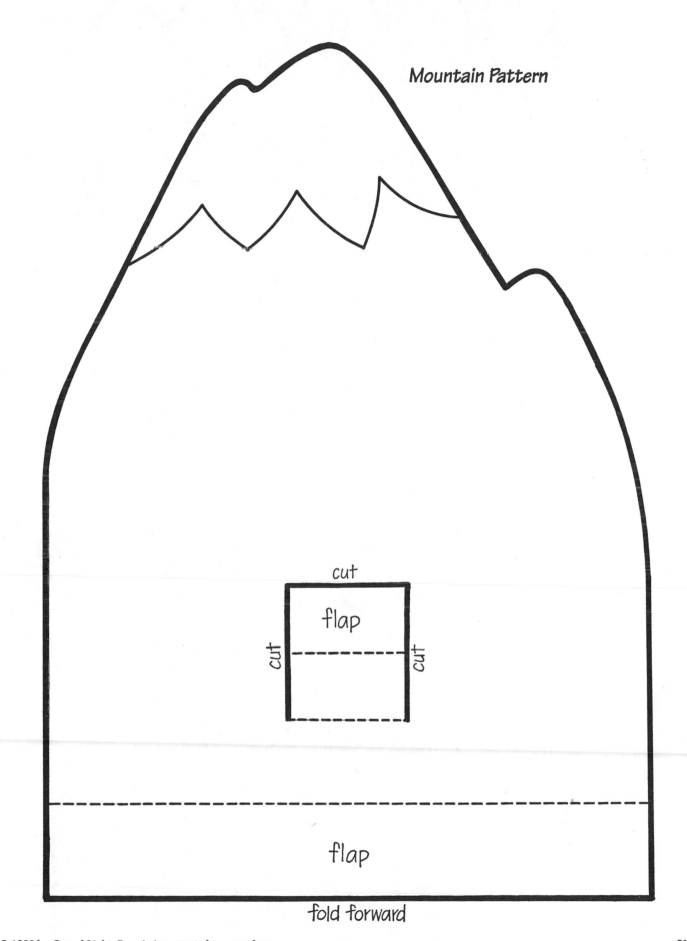

Mountain Pattern

cut

flap

cut

cut

flap

fold forward

51

Trees Pattern

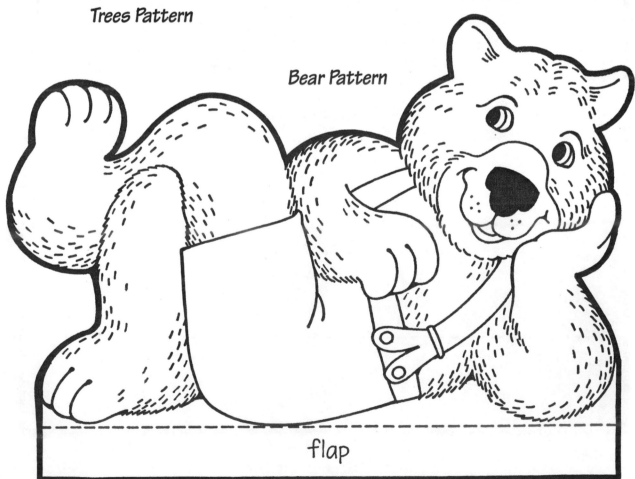

Bear Pattern

flap

Somethin' Fishy Wrist Game

(ONE- OR TWO-DAY PROJECT/60 MINUTES)

Materials: Game Board Pattern, white card-stock paper, lightweight cardboard, scissors, ruler, pencils, clear acetate or plastic (from bakery containers, deli containers, pasta boxes, etc.), hole punch, tacky glue, felt pens, photocopier. For each student—one small yogurt lid, three chenille wires in various colors, five round 3mm beads.

Preparation: Photocopy Game Board Pattern onto card stock—one for each student. Cut plastic into 4-inch (10-cm) squares—one for each student. Cut the lightweight cardboard into 4-inch (10-cm) squares—one for each student.

Instruct each student in the following procedures:
- Color the Game Board and cut out.
- Punch holes where indicated on Game Board.
- Glue Game Board to top side of the yogurt lid. (Use glue sparingly or Game Board will be bumpy.)
- Place yogurt lid on cardboard square, top side up. Trace and cut out.
- Fold cardboard circle in half and cut two slits (sketch a).
- Open circle and thread chenille wires through slits, laying them side by side (sketch b).
- Twist chenille wires together or braid them. Fold ends under to secure.

- Trace around top side of yogurt lid onto plastic square and cut out.
- Place five beads on Game Board.
- Carefully spread glue on rim of lid. Place plastic circle on rim.
- Turn yogurt lid over. Glue cardboard circle with chenille wires to the back of the lid. Let dry in this position.
- Place the game on wrist and twist the chenille wires to fit. Moving your wrist from side to side, try to get a bead in every hole—without the others falling out!

Simplification Idea: Teacher traces and cuts out plastic and cardboard circles beforehand.

Outdoor Life: **What percent of the earth's surface do you think is covered with water?** (More than seventy percent.) **Nearly all of this water is inhabited by fishes. What are some of the places where fish can be found?** (Oceans, streams, river, lakes.) **You might be surprised to know that fish also live in volcanic springs, foul swamps, and acid lakes. Some fishes even make temporary pools their homes, and when these pools dry up, the fishes either travel overland to find water elsewhere or hole up in mud until rains come; they may also die, but leave their drought-resistant eggs behind to carry on the race.**

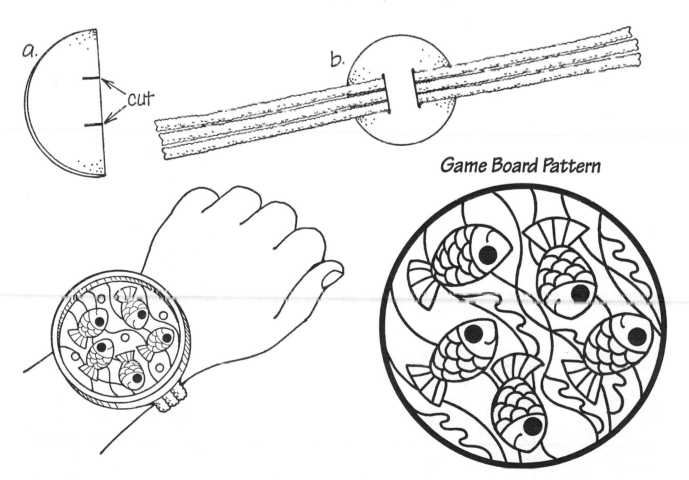

Game Board Pattern

Nature Checkers Game

(ONE- OR TWO-DAY PROJECT/60 MINUTES)

Materials: Construction paper (in a variety of colors), measuring stick, white foam core (available at graphic art supply stores) or white poster board, craft glue, acrylic paint in a variety of colors, small paintbrushes, pencils, shallow containers, paper cutter. For each student—24 flat, round stones approximately 1-inch (2.5-cm) in diameter, one zip-lock plastic sandwich bag. (If stones are not available, checkers can be made from self-drying clay.) Optional—clear self-adhesive paper.

Preparation: Cut foam core or poster board into 12-inch (30-cm) squares—one for each student. Use a paper cutter to cut 1¹/₂-inch (3.75-cm) squares from construction paper—64 for each student (32 of one color and 32 of another color). Optional: Cut self-adhesive paper into 12-inch (30-cm) squares—one for each student.

Instruct each student in the following procedures:

- To make checkers: Choose two simple nature designs to paint on your game pieces (such as a sun, mountain, tree, cloud, etc.). Paint 12 stones with one design and the remaining 12 stones with another design. Let dry.

- To make game board: Choose two colors of construction paper squares to use for your game board. Glue squares onto foam core in checkerboard design. Leave a small amount of white space between each of the squares and a ¹/₂-inch (1.25-cm) border around the outside edges.

- Optional: Cover game board with clear self-adhesive paper.

- On back side of each stone, paint a nature symbol that will be shown when the checker becomes a "king." Paint the same symbol on all 24 checkers. Let dry.

- Store checkers in zip-lock bag.

- Play game using traditional checkers game rules or play "Pinch Checkers." To play "Pinch Checkers": Place all checkers on same color squares. Pieces are moved diagonally, as in the traditional game, and may jump over opponent's checkers, however, a jumped checker is not removed from the board. A player takes an opponent's checker off the board only when he or she "pinches" the checker. That happens when the player traps his or her opponent's checker between two of his or her own checkers. There are no Kings. When a checker gets to the King's row (the opponent's back row), it stays there. The winner is the player who gets the most checkers to the King's row.

Enrichment Idea: Use black felt pen to outline painted designs on checkers.

Outdoor Life: **What kind of toys do you own? What do you think they're made of? Toys are made from materials that are taken out of the earth. When we buy toys that we don't use or that break easily and are then thrown away, we are wasting the earth's materials. What are some ways you can help conserve the earth's materials?** (Buying well-made toys that will last a long time; giving our old toys to other students, etc.) **Another way to conserve the earth's materials is to make toys out of things we already have, like we are doing today.**

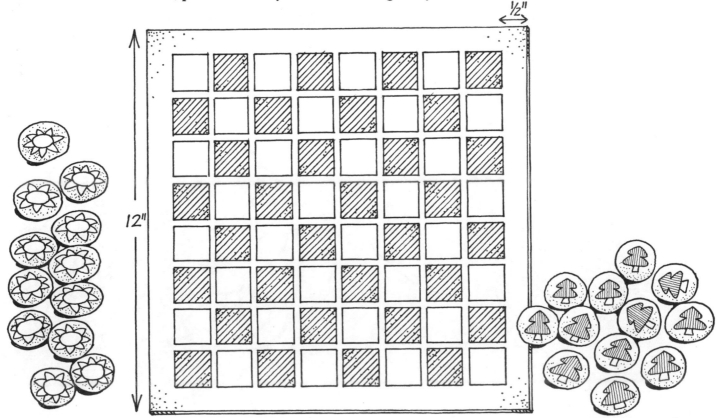

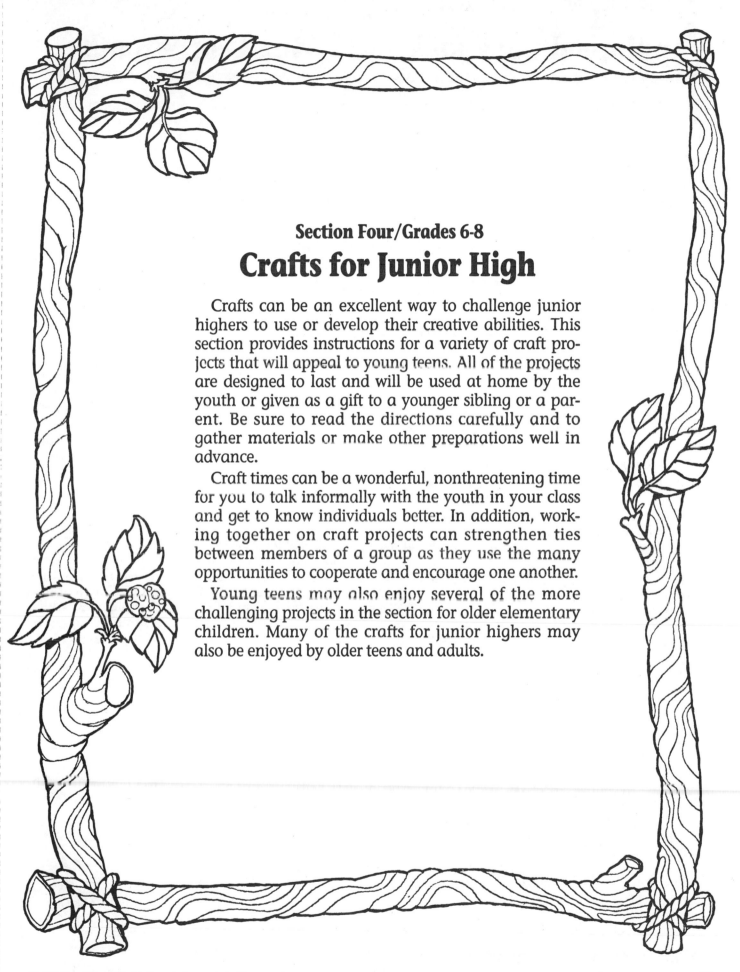

Section Four/Grades 6-8
Crafts for Junior High

Crafts can be an excellent way to challenge junior highers to use or develop their creative abilities. This section provides instructions for a variety of craft projects that will appeal to young teens. All of the projects are designed to last and will be used at home by the youth or given as a gift to a younger sibling or a parent. Be sure to read the directions carefully and to gather materials or make other preparations well in advance.

Craft times can be a wonderful, nonthreatening time for you to talk informally with the youth in your class and get to know individuals better. In addition, working together on craft projects can strengthen ties between members of a group as they use the many opportunities to cooperate and encourage one another.

Young teens may also enjoy several of the more challenging projects in the section for older elementary children. Many of the crafts for junior highers may also be enjoyed by older teens and adults.

Appliquéd Backpack
(TWO-DAY PROJECT/60 MINUTES EACH DAY)

Note: This craft requires a simple fabric backpack for each student. For backpack materials and sewing instructions see page 7.

Materials: Various colors and designs of cotton fabric, lightweight fusible interfacing with peel-off backing (such as Wonder-Under), squeeze tubes of dimensional fabric paint in several colors (available at fabric or craft supply stores), iron, ironing board, scissors, ruler, pencils, scratch paper. For each student—one backpack.

Preparation: Wash and dry all fabric to preshrink. Cut fabric into pieces 10-inches square or smaller. Cut interfacing to size of fabric and iron to fuse together.

Instruct each student in the following procedures:
DAY ONE:
• On scratch paper, draw scene or design you will create on your backpack.
• Copy elements of design onto various fabric pieces (fused with interfacing) and cut out.

DAY TWO:
• Peel paper backing off cut-out design pieces. Position design pieces on front side of backpack with fabric side up.
• Use iron to fuse design pieces onto backpack.
• Trace around all design pieces with dimensional paints. Let dry.

Enrichment Idea: Students choose an endangered plant, bird or animal to use as design on backpack. Students decorate backpack with a message about protecting the earth and its inhabitants.

Outdoor Life: How many of you walked or rode your bike at least once this week, instead of riding in a car? Good for you! Every time a car is driven, it burns gas and produces exhaust. (That's what you see coming out of the tail pipe.) Exhaust contains invisible gases that pollute the air. Let your backpack be a reminder that when we don't drive cars, we keep our earth a cleaner, healthier place to live.

cotton fabric   dimensional paint

Wax Leaf Wreath
(ONE-DAY PROJECT/60 MINUTES)

Materials: Cardboard, ruler, pencils, craft knife or scissors, assortment of pressed leaves, acorns or tiny pinecones, wax paper, newspapers, water, doubler boiler, small foil pans (potpie size), hot pads, spoons, stove or hot plate. For each student—one gummed picture hanger and approximately 1 cup of wax.

Preparation: Draw a 10-inch (25-cm) circle onto cardboard and cut out. Draw a 7½-inch (18.75-cm) circle in the center of the 10-inch (25-cm) circle and cut out to make wreath base—one for each student. Cover work area with newspapers. Place wax in foil pans. Set foil pan in double boiler and heat to melt wax. Set foil pans of melted wax in center of work area. (You may need to reheat and add more wax periodically.)

Instruct each student in the following procedures:
• Lay wreath base on a sheet of wax paper.
• Spoon a line of wax onto a section of the wreath base.
• Before wax on base hardens, hold a leaf by the stem, dip it into pan of melted wax until completely covered, then lay on waxed area of base (sketch a). Wax will hold leaves on cardboard.
• Continue adding wax and leaves until base is completely covered. Build up layers of leaves for a three-dimensional effect.
• Dip acorns or tiny pinecones into wax and lay on wreath to add a finishing touch.
• Allow wreath to cool, then peel away wax paper.
• Apply a gummed picture hanger to back of wreath.

Outdoor Life: Do you know why the leaves of some trees change color? Leaves are green because they contain a pigment called chlorophyll. The leaf also contains smaller quantities of other pigments which are hidden by the chlorophyll. As autumn approaches, the shorter days and cooler nights cause the chlorophyll to break down and the hidden colors of the leaf appear. The green pigment in evergreen trees is so hardy that it isn't affected by winter conditions.

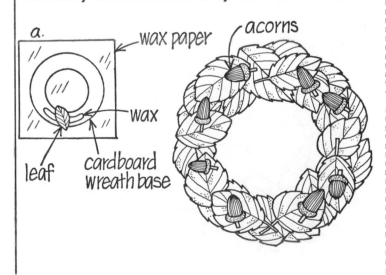

a.   wax paper   acorns   wax   leaf   cardboard wreath base

Granite Bookends

(TWO-DAY PROJECT/60 MINUTES)

Materials: Newspaper, scissors, heavy cardboard, flour, water, measuring cup, large bowl, spoon, shallow containers, aluminum foil, masking tape, old toothbrushes, paintbrushes, craft sticks, sand, funnel, pencil, several large cardboard boxes, craft knife, black and white acrylic craft paint, clear acrylic spray, paint shirts. For each student—two empty, individual-size juice boxes, two paper plates.

Preparation: FOR DAY ONE: Cut cardboard into 2¹/₂x4-inch (6.25x10-cm) rectangles—two for each student. Use a pencil to enlarge the straw holes in each juice box. Insert funnel in holes and fill boxes with sand. Tape holes closed. Cut newspapers into 1-inch (2.5-cm) strips of varying lengths. To make papier-mâché mixture: Combine one part flour with two parts water and mix until smooth. Pour mixture into shallow containers. FOR DAY 2: Combine some of the black and white paint to make gray. Reserve some white and black paint for spattering. (Note: Depending on the consistency of the paint, you may need to add a small amount of water in order to get a good spray when spattering. Be careful not to over-dilute the paint or the spatters will run.) Pour paint into containers. Make spattering stations out of cardboard boxes by cutting out a large "window" in the side of each box (sketch a). Set boxes outside if possible. Cover work area with newspapers.

Instruct each student in the following procedures:

DAY ONE:

- Tape each juice box upright onto a cardboard rectangle, forming an L shape (sketch b).
- Crumple pieces of foil. Press them together and tape them to juice box, making the form of a rock. Make the rock shape irregular for a realistic appearance. Leave the inside L shape of the bookend smooth (sketch c).
- Repeat for second bookend.

- Dip a newspaper strip into the papier-mâché mixture. Pull strip between fingers to remove excess mixture. Wrap strip around bookend. Continue adding strips until bookend is completely covered.
- Repeat for the second bookend.
- Allow to dry overnight.

DAY TWO:

- Place each bookend on a paper plate.
- Paint each bookend completely with gray paint.
- At the spattering station, place plate and bookend inside the box.
- Dip a toothbrush in the black paint. Holding the toothbrush bristle-side down, a few inches away from the bookend, run craft stick along the bristles, allowing the paint to spray and spatter your project. Always keep the toothbrush facing away from you and work inside the box.
- Turn the paper plate as you spatter the bookend to cover the surface evenly.
- Spatter bookend again with the white paint.
- Repeat process to spatter second bookend.
- Allow to dry.
- Spray with clear acrylic spray.

Enrichment Idea: Use a third color of acrylic paint in the spattering process. This will give each project a more unique look.

Outdoor Life: What is granite? Granite is a hard, coarse-grained rock that makes up a large part of every continent. It's usually white, pink or light gray in color. Granite is strong and durable and is useful in the construction of buildings. Granite can also be polished smooth, making it a popular material for building columns, tombstones and monuments. What have you seen that is made from granite?

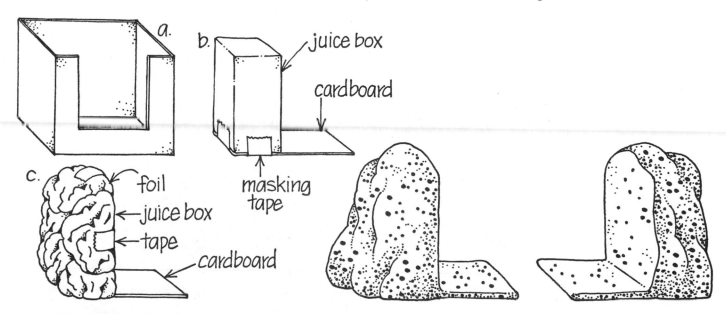

a.

b. juice box

cardboard

c. foil

juice box

tape

cardboard

masking tape

Dried Flower Swag

(ONE OR TWO-DAY PROJECT/60 MINUTES)

Materials: Assorted dried long-stemmed flowers, grasses and weeds (see "Drying and Pressing Leaves and Flowers," p. 8), heavy scissors or pruning shears, fine-gauge wire, measuring stick, pliers, 2-inch (5-cm) wide ribbon, clear acrylic spray.

Preparations: Cut ribbon into 3-foot (90-cm) lengths—one for each student. Cut wire into 6-inch (15-cm) lengths—two for each student.

Instruct each student in the following procedures:

- Select a combination of dried flowers, weeds and grasses for swag.
- Arrange materials in two identical sprays with stems intermingled in the center. Wire sprays together (sketch a). Twist wire with pliers to pull taut.
- Fill in bare spots by adding individual sprigs as needed.
- Take complete swag outside and lightly spray with clear acrylic spray as a preservative.
- To make bow: Loop ribbon in a loose oval approximately 6 inches (15 cm) long (sketch b).
- Flatten oval and cut a 1/2-inch (1.25-cm) "v" on either side (sketch c). Wrap wire around "v" and twist wire tightly in back of ribbon. Leave ends of wire long.
- Pull out individual ribbon loops and twist them until bow is full and rounded.
- Pull out ends of ribbon and cut them at an angle.
- Tie long ends of wire around middle of dried arrangement.

Outdoor Life: When you are taking a hike, is it OK to pick wildflowers? In the United States, about ten percent of all native flowering plants are so rare they are considered to be endangered species. Unless these plants are protected in their natural surroundings, they may die out completely. The government has passed laws that prohibit people from picking wildflowers in public parks and forests. What are some ways we might enjoy wildflowers without picking them? Before picking wildflowers, make sure they are abundant in the area and you have permission from the owner of the property.

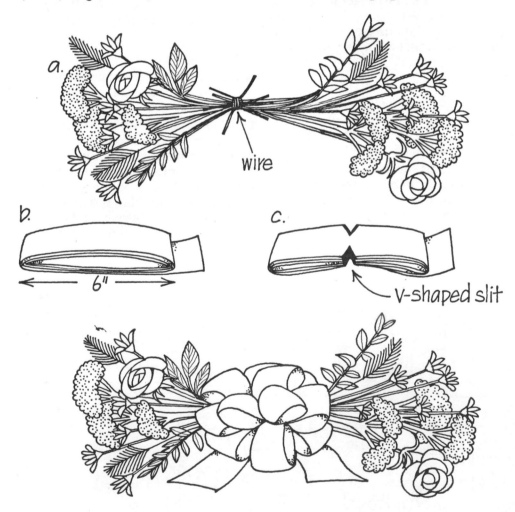

a.

wire

b.

6"

c.

v-shaped slit

Molded Sawdust Animal

(ONE-DAY PROJECT/30 MINUTES)

Materials: Sawdust, wheat flour (not self-rising), water, measuring spoon, measuring cup, mixing spoon, large sauce pan, stove, pine or other nature-scented oil, aluminum foil, shallow containers for water. Optional—sandpaper, clear acrylic spray.

Preparation: To make molding compound: Place 2/3 cup wheat flour in a saucepan. Gradually add 2 cups water, stirring to break up lumps. Place pan over low heat and continue stirring until mixture is somewhat clear. Remove from stove and add 1/2 teaspoon scented oil. Stir until well blended. Add 2 cups sawdust and blend until thoroughly mixed. (Recipe makes enough for four fist-sized objects.) Cut a piece of aluminum foil for each student to work on. Set out shallow containers of water.

Instruct each student in the following procedures:
- Mold material into the shape of an animal or other object (Model as you would with any clay.) Bits of the modeling compound may be added by moistening with water and adhering to figure.
- Air dry sculptures for 2-3 days or bake in an oven at 200 degrees. Oven drying time will vary with thickness of object.
- Optional: When completely dry, sand object and spray with clear acrylic spray for a more finished look.

Enrichment Idea: Check out several library books containing pictures of wildlife. Students look at illustrations in books to get ideas for their projects.

Outdoor Life: Invite volunteers to describe the characteristics of their favorite animals as others guess what they are describing. **How would you feel if your favorite animal became extinct—disappeared from the earth? Every day, there are more people living on the earth, moving into places that are homes for plants and animals. As a result, each week about 20 kinds of plants and animals become extinct. A few of the animals that are currently in danger of extinction are the Asiatic lion, brown bear, zebra, elephant, elk and rhinoceros. Some zoos, parks and other organizations are taking steps to protect these endangered species. Contact your local zoo to see how you can help.**

Pinecone Basket

(ONE- OR TWO-DAY PROJECT/60 MINUTES)

Materials: Wire cutters or tin snips, 18- or 20-inch (45- or 50-cm) gauge floral wire. For each student—approximately 50 small pinecones approximately 1 1/2x3/4 inches (3.75x1.9 cm), one pint-size plastic berry basket.

Preparation: Cut wire into 2-foot (60-cm) lengths—one for each student.

Instruct each student in the following procedures:
- Working up from the bottom of basket, screw a pinecone into each window (sketch a).
- To make handle: Bend wire in half. Place fold of wire around pinecone in center of the basket's top row. Twist wire several times to secure it to the pinecone.
- Add pinecones one at a time to the handle, placing a pinecone between the wires, then twisting the wires to secure (sketch b).
- Bend wire to form an arch. Finish handle by bringing the two wire ends around the center pinecone opposite the one with which you started.
- Twist wire ends together and tuck underneath pinecone.

Outdoor Life: **How many different kinds of pinecones do you think one pine tree bears? Pine trees bear both male and female cones. The male cones are usually less than one inch (2.5 cm) in length. The female cones are much larger and usually have woody scales. The male cones produce pollen, which is carried by the wind to egg cells attached to the scales of female cones. The pollen fertilizes the egg cells, which then develop into seeds. The seeds are blown to the spot where they will land and grow into pine trees.**

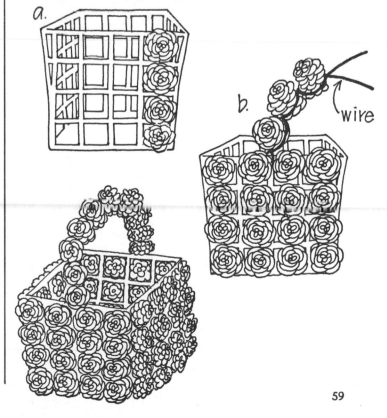

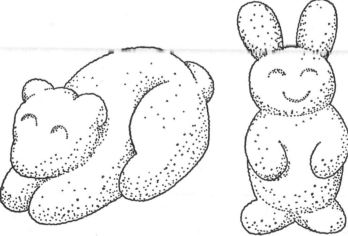

Weather Stone

(ONE-DAY PROJECT/30 MINUTES)

Materials: Scissors, craft glue, twine, measuring stick, acrylic paints, small paintbrushes, shallow containers, black fine-tip felt pens, newspaper, transparent tape, paper, photocopier. For each student—one sturdy stick approximately 2 feet (.6 m) in length, one fist-sized stone.

Preparation: Photocopy "The Amazing Weather Stone"—one copy for each student. Cover work area with newspapers. Cut twine into 2½-foot (75-cm) lengths—one for each student. Pour paint into shallow containers.

Instruct each student in the following procedures:

- Squeeze a line of glue around center of stone. Wrap one end of twine several times around center of stone and tie securely.
- Squeeze a line of glue around one end of stick about 2 inches (5 cm) from end. Wrap other end of twine several times around glued section and tie securely.
- Paint weather symbols on stone, such as lightning bolts, rain clouds, sun. Allow to dry.
- Outline the designs and draw details with fine-tip felt pens.

Enrichment Idea: Students go on a nature hike to collect sticks and stones.

Outdoor Life: Invite students to guess where in the world these weather extremes were recorded:

Highest temperature recorded— 136° F at Al Aziziyah, Libya on September 13, 1922.

Lowest temperature recorded— -128.6° F at Vostok Station in Antarctica on July 21, 1983.

Strongest winds recorded— Mount Washington, New Hampshire on April 12, 1934. The wind blew at 188 mph (303 kph) for five minutes. One gust reached 231 mph (372 kph).

Heaviest rainfall recorded— in Cilaos on the Island of Reunion in the Indian Ocean. It rained 73.62 inches (186.99 cm) in 24 hours on March 15,16, 1952.

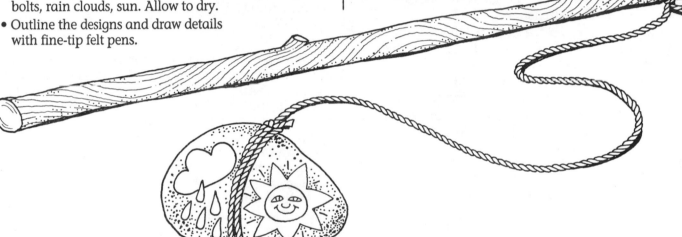

The Amazing Weather Stone

You may have heard about the fad from several years ago when *everyone* wanted to be the first in their neighborhood to adopt a "pet rock." Well, now you have the honor of being the first in your neighborhood to own the Amazing Weather Stone! This handy device takes the guesswork out of knowing how to dress and what plans you can make for each day. Just think—no more picnics in the rain and no more snow boots in sunny, sweltering weather. You will no longer need to depend on the weatherperson's predictions for the daily weather. (And how often are their predictions accurate anyway?!!) Your friends and neighbors will wonder why you're so much smarter than the weatherperson. Here's the secret...to find out what kind of weather it is, simply follow these easy instructions:

✳ Stand outside and hold the end of the stick so the stone dangles from the end of the string.

✳ If the stone is gently SWAYING...it's BREEZY!

✳ If the stone is SWINGING...it's WINDY!

✳ If the stone is WET...it's RAINING!

✳ If the stone is WARM and DRY...it's SUNNY!

✳ If the stone is MOIST...it's HUMID!

✳ If the stone is DIFFICULT TO SEE...it's FOGGY!

✳ If the stone is COVERED BY SHADOWS...it's CLOUDY!

✳ If the stone is WHITE...it's SNOWING!

✳ If the stone is SPINNING IN CIRCLES... it's either a TORNADO or a HURRICANE (depending on where you live)!

✳ If the stone is SHAKING...it's an EARTHQUAKE!

Now, aren't you glad you're the proud owner of a weather stone?!!

Forest Frame

(TWO-DAY PROJECT/30 MINUTES EACH DAY)

Materials: Earth tone air-drying clay (available at art supply and hobby stores), instant camera and film, newspapers, narrow ribbon or sturdy string, scissors, pencils, cardboard, small nature items (tiny pinecones, petals from larger pinecones, dried pine needles, dried weeds, straw flowers, seed pods, pebbles, etc.), burlap scraps, tacky glue. Optional—regular camera and film.

Preparation: Use instant camera to take a snapshot of each student (or use regular camera and have photos developed in time to be used for project). Or, ask students ahead of time to bring a photo they would like to frame. Cover work area with newspapers.

Instruct each student in the following procedures:

DAY ONE:
- Decide what size and shape frame to make. Below are ideas for several different types of frames. If photo was taken, frame should be made to fit the size of that photo. Keep in mind that clay will shrink slightly.
- To make a large oval frame: Roll clay into a long rope. Coil clay rope into an oval-shaped frame (sketch a). Pat the coils to flatten them into the desired shape.
- To make smaller frames: Model clay into the desired shape (circle, rectangle, square, pine tree, etc.), leaving a cut-out hole for picture.
- Gently press a piece of burlap against the clay, then remove burlap to create an interesting textured design in clay.
- Press small nature items into the clay to decorate frame (see sketch). Make sure the items are pressed deeply enough so that they don't fall out as the clay dries. (If

any items do loosen later, they can be glued back into place.)
- If making a small round frame, you may want to wrap a piece of ribbon around it to give it the look of a miniature wreath (see sketch).
- If making a small pine tree-shaped frame, make textured design by pressing pine needles into the clay (see sketch). Press miniature pinecones into the clay.
- Use a pencil to make a hole near the top of frame.
- Let frame dry. Smaller frames generally dry overnight. Larger frames take several days to dry thoroughly. Clay dries more quickly if placed in a sunny location.

DAY TWO:
- Glue photo behind opening of frame. Cut a piece of cardboard and glue it behind the photograph.
- To make picture hanger: Insert a piece of string or ribbon through hole at top of frame and tie ends securely together. If it is a large frame, make sure the ribbon or string is sturdy enough to hold the weight of the frame.

Outdoor Life: Which items in this room are made from materials that come from the forest? Forests are one of the riches of the earth. They are home to thousands of plants and animals and trees. Unfortunately, many forests are being destroyed as we cut down the trees for paper and other wood products. The average American uses seven trees a year! We can help save our beautiful forests by recycling paper and wood products. What are some paper or wood products we can recycle here in our classroom? At home? When we go shopping?

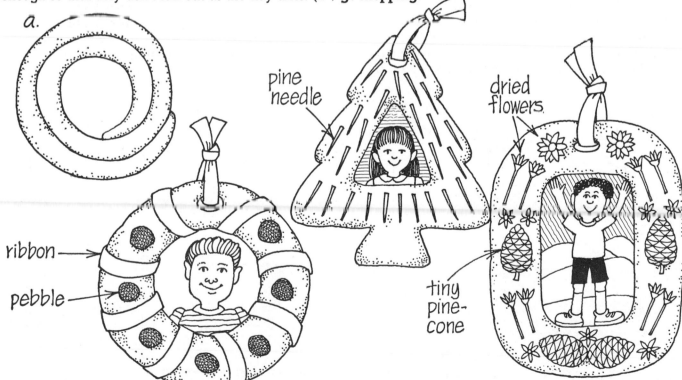

Pop-Up Butterfly

(TWO-DAY PROJECT/30 MINUTES EACH DAY)

Note: This project works best with a small group of students and may require more teacher assistance than usual. However, be assured that these simple materials combined with creativity and a little patience produce a delightful result in the Pop-Up Butterfly.

Materials: Butterfly Body, Right and Left Wings and Wing Support Patterns (pp. 63-65), white card stock paper, photocopier, pencils, black fine-tip markers, paper clips, glue, water, shallow containers, craft tissue in a variety of bright colors, scissors, paintbrushes, white poster board, measuring stick, craft knife, black chenille wire, newspapers, heavy books for weights.

Preparation: Photocopy Butterfly Patterns onto white card stock—one set for each student. Cut tissue paper into various shapes, 1 inch (2.5 cm) and smaller. Thin glue with water (two parts glue, one part water) and pour into shallow containers. Cut chenille wire into 6-inch (15-cm) lengths—one for each student. Cut poster board into 11x14-inch (27.5x35-cm) sheets—one for each student. Cover work area with newspaper.

Instruct each student in the following procedures:
DAY ONE:

• Cut out all Butterfly Patterns on solid lines.

• Fold Back Wing Flaps back and glue to underside of wings. Use paper clips to hold together until dry.

• Dip paintbrush in thinned glue and "paint" a wing. Lay tissue pieces over glue to create a design (sketch a). Repeat to cover both sides of all four wings and one side of body.

DAY TWO:

• Fold poster board in half widthwise to crease and then open again.

• Use scissors to cut slits in Bottom Wings where indicated. Slide the two wings together along slits (sketch b).

• Fold tabs down and glue on either side of fold line on poster board (sketch c). Note: The tabs at the head end of your butterfly should touch the fold and the tabs at the tail end should adhere about 1/2-inch (1.25-cm) away from the fold. Carefully fold poster board closed with the butterfly in place. Place a heavy book on top and allow to dry.

• Set Butterfly Body on a pad of newspapers and use craft knife to cut slits where indicated.

• Fold Body in half lengthwise. Use pencil to poke a hole for antennae through both thicknesses where indicated. Insert chenille wire through holes. Twist together near Body and curl at ends to form antennae (sketch d). Fold tabs down along fold lines.

• Fold Top Wing tabs back along fold lines. Insert tabs into slits on Body. Glue tabs to underside of Body. Secure with paper clips and allow to dry.

• Open poster board and Back Wing assemblage. Squeeze a small line of glue along bottom of Body tabs. Set tabs onto either side of Back wing assemblage.

• Fold Wing Supports into "U" shapes along fold lines. Squeeze glue along tabs and attach between top and bottom wings. Base of "U" shape should be facing away from the Butterfly Body. Secure with paper clips and allow to dry.

Simplification Idea: Add color to the butterfly with felt markers rather than using the tissue paper technique.

Outdoor Life: Check out a library book containing photographs of butterflies. Students refer to photos to get ideas for decorating their Pop-Up Butterflies. **Have you ever wondered where a butterfly goes when it rains? The tiny bodies of butterflies are very sensitive to changes in weather. When it's raining, they take shelter under leaves on plants or trees. On very hot days, butterflies keep cool by sipping water and resting in the shade. Most butterflies live for only a few weeks during the spring and summer.**

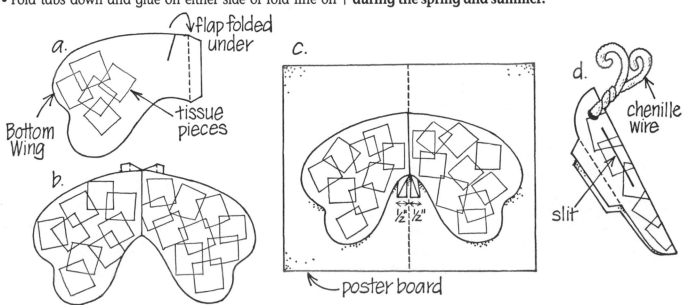

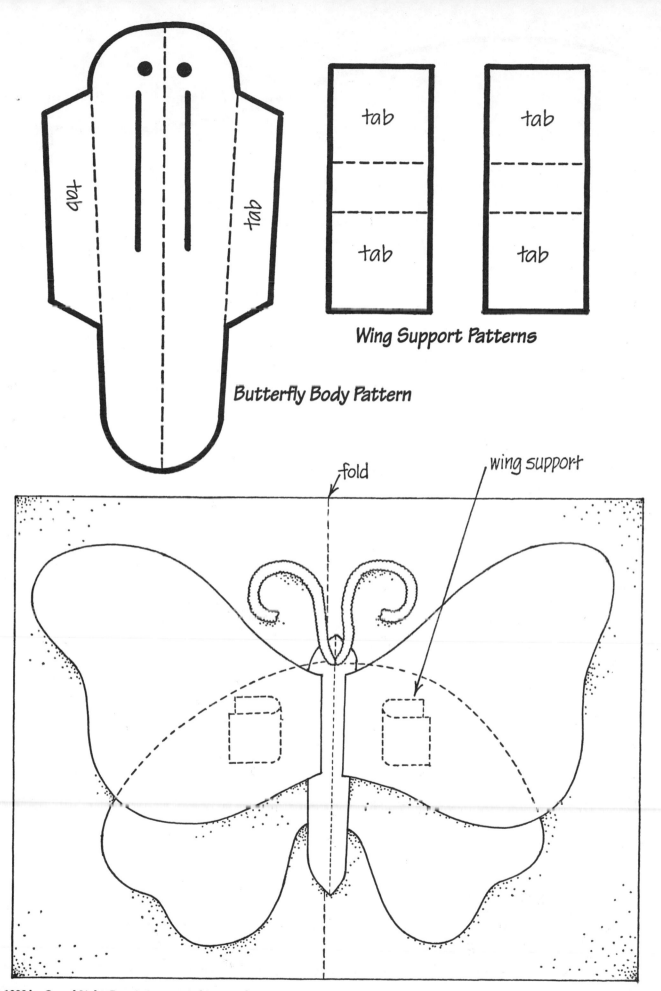

tab

tab

tab

Wing Support Patterns

tab

tab

Butterfly Body Pattern

fold

wing support

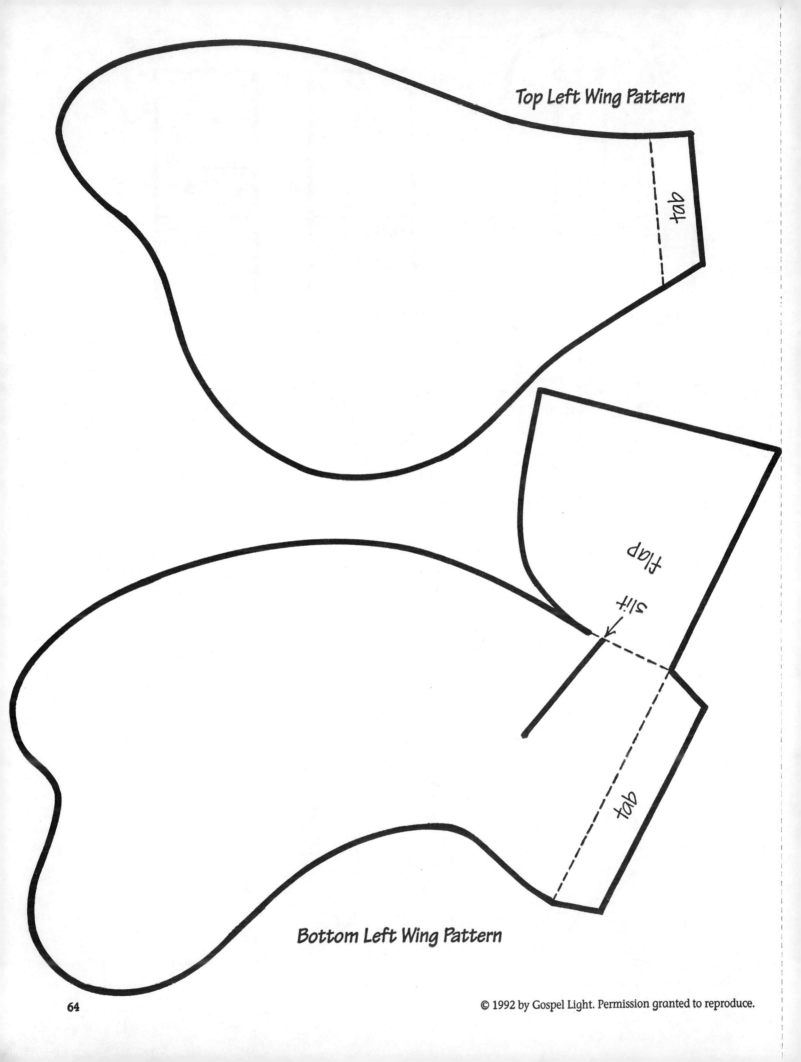

Top Left Wing Pattern

tab

flap

slit

tab

Bottom Left Wing Pattern

64

© 1992 by Gospel Light. Permission granted to reproduce.

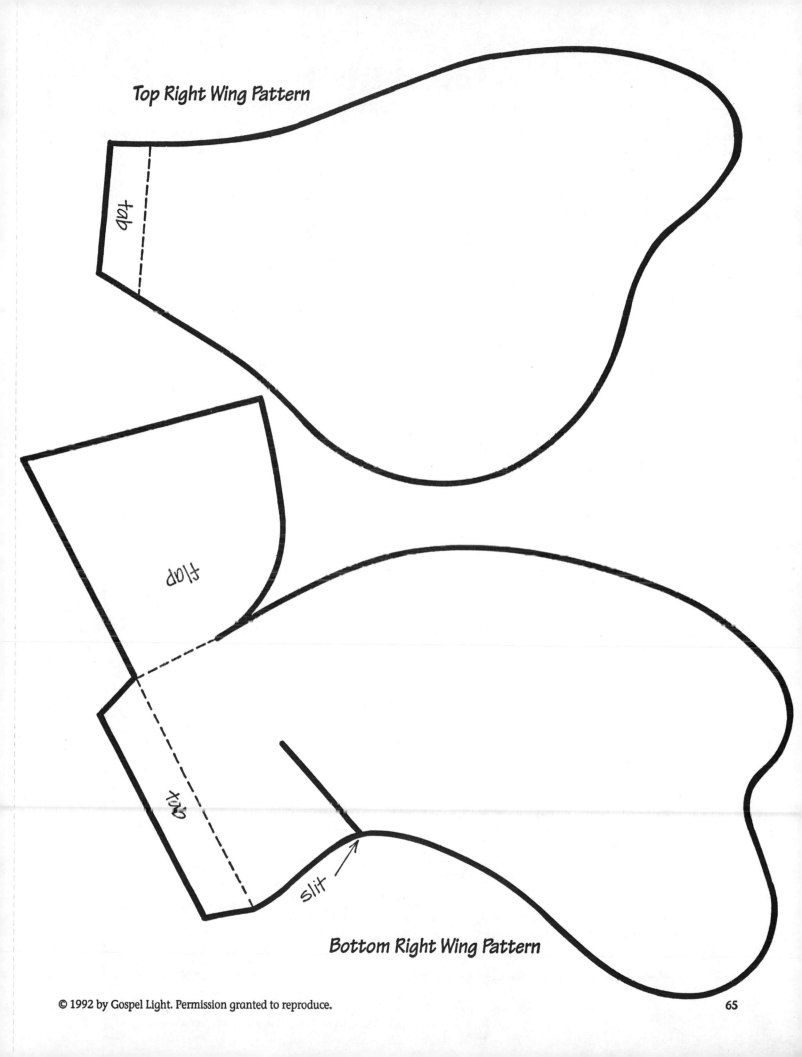

Top Right Wing Pattern

tab

flap

tab

slit

Bottom Right Wing Pattern

Lashed Trivet

(ONE- OR TWO-DAY PROJECT/60 MINUTES)

Materials: Pruning shears, sticks approximately ½ inch (1.25 cm) in diameter (pussy willows work well). For each student—one pair of 72-inch (1.8-m) leather boot laces (or plastic craft lace or sturdy string).

Preparation: Use pruning shears to cut sticks into 9-inch (22.5-cm) lengths—eighteen for each student.

Instruct each student in the following procedures:

- Select the two straightest and sturdiest sticks to use as support sticks, then set aside.
- Fold leather laces in half and lay on table about 6 inches (15 cm) apart. Lay a stick across laces near loops (sketch a). Bring ends of each lace over stick and through loops to make "cow hitches" (sketch b).
- Place one support stick through each lace loop perpendicular to the first stick (sketch c). Pull laces tight.
- Cross lace ends to make an *X* over each support stick (sketch d).

- Place another stick under support sticks and on top of laces (sketch e).
- Repeat prior two steps to add sticks until there is a total of 16 sticks laced to the support sticks. (Pull the laces very tight as you push the cross sticks closely together.)
- After adding the last stick, tie laces in square knots (sketch f) and trim ends.

Outdoor Life: Do you know how to tell the age of a tree? Most trees grow a layer of wood each year. After such a tree has been cut down, the layers can be seen as rings in the trunk. These annual rings reveal the tree's life story. Narrow center rings may indicate that other trees shaded the tree when it was young, depriving it of moisture and sunlight. Wider rings may indicate the surrounding trees were cut down and the tree received lots of sunlight and moisture during a specific time in it's life.

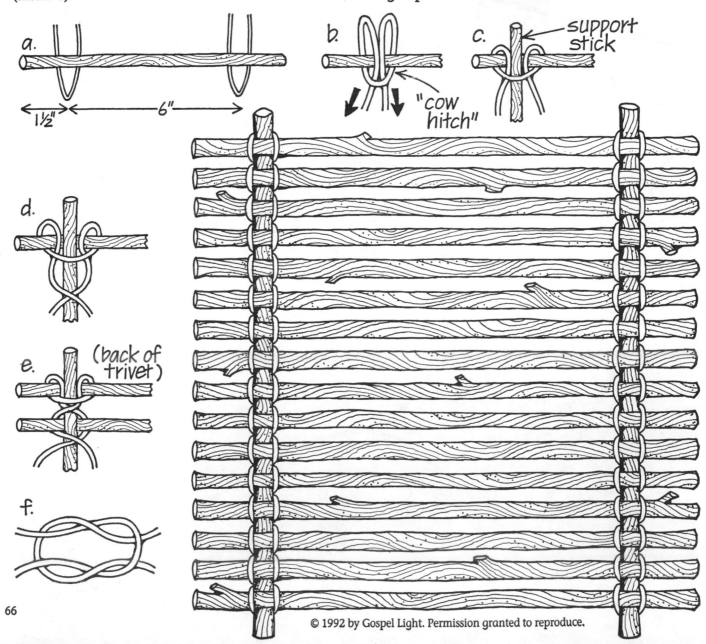

Reproducible Pages

Bible Memory Verse Coloring Posters

The following pages are reproducible and contain ten Bible Memory Verse designs for younger elementary children and ten for older elementary children. Ideas for using these pages include:

1. Use the photocopied pages as rewards for children who memorize the Bible verse. They may take the page home to color and display.

2. Photocopy a set of coloring posters for each student. Cover with a folded sheet of construction paper and staple to make a coloring book.

3. Use the pages in class for transition times or for students who finish an activity ahead of other students.

4. Play a coloring game. Place a variety of felt pens on the table. Recite the verse together. Then each student may choose a pen and use it to color on his or her page for one minute. When time is up, students put pens down and repeat verse together again. Students then choose another pen and color for one minute. Repeat process until pages are completed or students tire of activity.

5. To customize pages, cover the Bible verse with white paper and letter another verse or saying in its place before you photocopy.

Student Certificates and Awards

The awards and certificates on the following pages may be personalized for various uses. Just follow these simple procedures:

1. Tear out certificate and letter the name of your program on the appropriate line.

2. Photocopy as many copies of certificate as needed.

3. Letter each child's certificate with his or her name (and achievement when appropriate).

Sticker Posters

1. Photocopy a sticker poster for each student.

2. After students color posters, attach them to a wall or bulletin board.

3. Students add stickers to their posters each day as they arrive. Or you may want to use stickers as rewards for reciting Bible memory verses, being helpful, or completing assignments.

"For the Lord gives wisdom, and from his mouth come knowledge and understanding." Proverbs 2:6

"He who walks with the wise grows wise, but a companion of fools suffers harm." Proverbs 13:20

"A prudent man gives thought to his steps."
Proverbs 14:15

"Listen to advice and accept instruction, and in the end you will be wise."
Proverbs 19:20

Younger Elementary
Coloring Page 4

"He who despises his neighbor sins, but blessed is he who is kind to the needy." Proverbs 14:21

"A gentle answer turns away wrath, but a harsh word stirs up anger." Proverbs 15:1

"Lazy hands make a man poor, but diligent hands bring wealth." Proverbs 10:4

Younger Elementary Coloring Page 7

"Do not withhold good from those who deserve it, when it is in your power to act." Proverbs 3:27

"There is deceit in the hearts of those who plot evil, but joy for those who promote peace." Proverbs 12:20

"Trust in the Lord with all your heart...and he will make your paths straight." Proverbs 3:5,6

Younger Elementary Coloring Page 10

"For the Lord gives wisdom, and from his mouth come knowledge and understanding." Proverbs 2:6

"He who walks with the wise grows wise, but a companion of fools suffers harm."
Proverbs 13:20

Older Elementary
Coloring Page 2

"A simple man believes anything, but a prudent man gives thought to his steps." Proverbs 14:15

Older Elementary Coloring Page 3
© 1992 by Gospel Light. Permission granted to reproduce.

"Listen to advice and accept instruction, and in the end you will be wise." Proverbs 19:20

Older Elementary
Coloring Page 4

"He who despises his neighbor sins, but blessed is he who is kind to the needy." Proverbs 14:21

"A gentle answer turns away wrath, but a harsh word stirs up anger." Proverbs 15:1

"Lazy hands make a man poor, but diligent hands bring wealth." Proverbs 10:4

"Do not withhold good from those who deserve it, when it is in your power to act." Proverbs 3:27

"There is deceit in the hearts of those who plot evil, but joy for those who promote peace." Proverbs 12:20

Older Elementary Coloring Page 9
© 1992 by Gospel Light. Permission granted to reproduce.

"Trust in the Lord with all your heart and lean not on your own understanding; in all your ways acknowledge him and he will make your paths straight." Proverbs 3:5,6

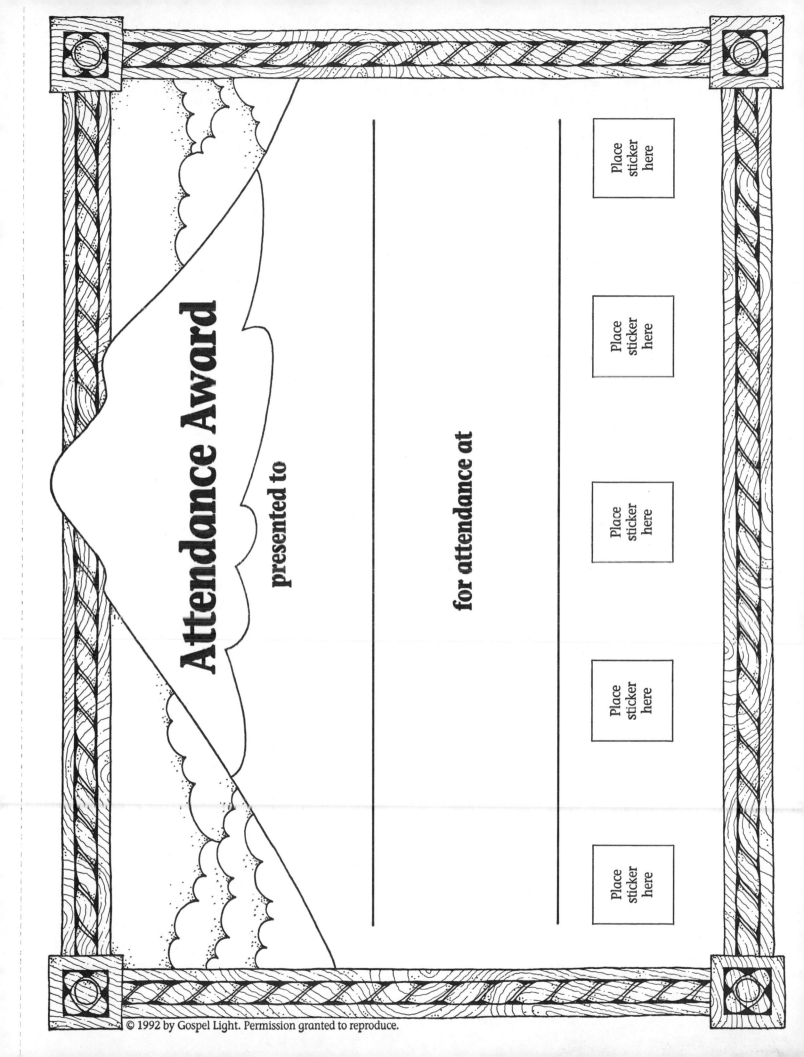

Attendance Award

presented to

for attendance at

Place sticker here

Place sticker here

Place sticker here

Place sticker here

Place sticker here

This is to certify that

_____

memorized all the Bible Memory Verses at

_____

_____

thanks so much for

_____

_____

_____

Good Friend Award

_____

was a good friend at

_____

© 1992 by Gospel Light. Permission granted to reproduce

Visitor Award

_____

we're glad you came to

_____

Please come back again!

Earth Buddy Award

_____

helped take care of the earth by

_____

_____

Flying Colors Award

_____

met a challenge with flying colors!

_____

_____

Sticker Poster

Index

Appliquéd Backpack 56

Backwoods Bug Jar 13

Bear Paw Stilts 28

Colored-Pebble Picture 19

Dried Flower Swag 58

Embossed Metal Magnets 48

Finger Puppets 26

Flowering Tiles 37

Forest Animal Hats 14

Forest Animal Mobile 40

Forest Frame 61

Granite Bookends 57

Helpless Hiker Paperweight 10

Ladybug Tic-Tac-Toe 24

Lashed Trivet 66

Leaf Place Mat 18

Leaf-Covered Box 47

Molded Sawdust Animal 59

Mountain View Diorama 42

  Background Scene 42

  Trees and Shrubs 43

  Tent and Campfire 43

  Beaver and Beaver Dam 44

  Fisherman and Canoe 44

Nature Checkers Game 54

Nature Collage Picture Frame 25

Nature Image Plaque 37

Nature Wall Hanging 19

Owl with Revolving Eyes 30

Pinecone Basket 59

Pinecone Rabbit 34

Plant a Tree! 20

Pop-Up Bear Card 50

Pop-Up Butterfly 62

Pop-Up Frog 38

Pressed Flower Sun Catcher 32

Raccoon Blinker 16

Really Neat Recycling Bins 48

Rickrack Backpack 36

Rock Campfire Scene 32

Rock Owl 14

Secret Stone 46

Somethin' Fishy Wrist Game 53

Spatter-Painted Bandana 26

Sponge-Painted Backpack 12

Stenciled Backpack 22

Tic-Tac-Toe Backpack 36

Tree Branch Frame 45

Twig Trees 12

Wax Leaf Wreath 56

Weather Stone 60